# BROTHERS
# TERENCE

Introduction and Translation
## Charles Mercier

University of Southern California

**Focus Classical Library**
**Focus Publishing/R Pullins Company**
**Newburyport MA 01950**

## The Focus Classical Library
### Series Editors • James Clauss and Michael Halleran

Hesiod's *Theogony* • Richard Caldwell • 1987
*The Heracles* of Euripides • Michael Halleran • 1988
Aristophanes' *Lysistrata* • Jeff Henderson • 1988
Sophocles' *Oedipus at Colonus* • Mary Whitlock Blundell • 1990
Euripides' *Medea* • Anthony Podlecki • 1991
Aristophanes' *Acharnians* • Jeff Henderson • 1992
Aristophanes' *The Clouds* • Jeff Henderson • 1992
*The Homeric Hymns* • Susan Shelmerdine • 1995
Aristophanes: *Acharnians, Lysistrata, Clouds* • Jeff Henderson • 1997
Euripides' *Bacchae* • Steve Esposito • 1998
Terence: *Brothers* • Charles Mercier • 1998

### The Focus Philosophical Library
### Series Editor • Albert Keith Whitaker

Plato's *Sophist* • E. Brann, P. Kalkavage, E. Salem • 1996
Plato's *Parmenides* • Albert Keith Whitaker • 1996
Plato's *Symposium* • Avi Sharon • 1998
Plato's *Phaedo* • E. Brann, P. Kalkavage, E. Salem • 1998

Cover: Detail of Mask. Second style frescoe. Room of the Masks. Domus Augustana, Palatine Hill, Rome, Italy. Scala/Art Resource, NY

Copyright © 1998 Charles Mercier

ISBN 0-941051-72-2

Printed in the United States of America
10 9 8 7 6 5 4 3 2 1

# Table of Contents

Preface

Introduction                                                            1

    Terence and the ancient comic tradition               1

    Production                                            7

    Terence's *Brothers*                                 10

    Suggestions for further reading                      16

    A video production of Terence's *Brothers*           17

Terence: *Brothers*                                                     23

# PREFACE

*Brothers* by Terence was first produced in Rome in Latin in 160 B.C.E. Its original title was not *Fratres*, but *Adelphoe* , the title of the Greek comedy by Menander that Terence here translates and adapts. Terence preferred Greek titles. This translation began as the script for a film of the play, the inaugural effort of the Terence Project. It was meant to be performed, and tries to communicate concretely the social realities the play represents and the trains of thoughts of its characters. It is in prose, not verse, but lines were divided to help the actors grasp rhetorical units. Rather than attempt to approximate in any way the original verse forms, it indicates the kind of delivery the original verse form implies, on which more in the introduction.

*Brothers* deals with questions of perennial interest: how best to raise children? how to give self-disinterested moral advice? It also presents elements that to an audience distanced by more than 2100 years may seem inappropriate to comedy. How funny is rape? How funny is slavery? The introduction, meant for those reading Terence for the first time, presents him not so much as intricate plotter or provider of holiday entertainment for an audience who wanted to leave their mental faculties at home (which I don't deny he was), but as a playwright writing in a comic tradition that enabled him to represent his city critically with some realism. Terence's comedies invite their audience to question the violence they occasionally represent: how funny the comedy may be is another matter. The introduction draws almost entirely from the work of others; it seemed best to forego formal acknowledgment of that in footnotes and instead invite exploration of the suggestions for further reading.

The translation is based for the most part on the Latin text of R. H. Martin (Cambridge, 1976).

I offer my thanks to Alexander Gombach, co-director and producer with me of the film, and the members of the cast, especially Paul Mercier and David Costabile; to my colleagues at Vassar College, Robert Brown, Margaret Fusco, and Rachel Kitzinger, who generously supported the film, and the student members of the seminar, Roman Comedy in Performance; to Kenneth Rothwell and Thomas Habinek for much helpful criticism (and who are absolved of responsibility for what remains); and Cynthia Zawalich for her careful editing.

Charles E. Mercier
Santa Monica, California

# Introduction

## Terence and the ancient comic tradition

What remains of Suetonius' early second century C.E. *Life of Terence* provides us the material to construct an appealing biography of Terence, though responsible critical assessment requires skepticism about these facts. If recent years have seen a lively interest in identifying African contributions to the cultural achievements of the Greeks and Romans and in appreciating the multiculturalism of the ancient Mediterranean, Terence is an intriguing figure. Plato and Cleopatra were not Africans, but Publius Terentius Afer, a foundational Western playwright, is said to have been. From Carthage in North Africa, he is brought as a slave to Rome and manumitted when his intellectual gifts are recognized by his politically prominent masters. He is an African writing translations and adaptations of Greek comedies into Latin for a Roman audience, a former slave, one for whom Greek and Latin are acquired languages. As for the color of Terence's skin, he is *colore fusco*, of dark color. Terence dies tragically young, of a broken heart, when years of work reading and translating in the dramatic archives of Athens went down in a shipwreck, a result understandable to anyone careless about keeping backup disks.

Without question, Terence died about 159 B.C.E., perhaps in his mid-thirties, sometime after the production of his last play, *Brothers*, and after a brilliant ten year career as a playwright patronized by the most sophisticated elements of Roman society. If we are not certain that he was born in Africa, or that he was a slave, we are in a position to speak with confidence of the relentless intelligence of his drama, whatever its origin. Six of his plays survive for us, and we see that his influence on the course of the literary Latin that follows him is decisive, similar to Shakespeare's on English. We can also locate him within the tradition in which he worked, that of Greek and Roman New Comedy.

The tradition of literary comedy in Athens and Rome has its ultimate origin in Homer's *Odyssey* (about 700 B.C.E.). The perspective of the *Odyssey* complements that of the *Iliad* by including concerns forbidden to the *Iliad's* stark heroism, the concerns of the belly. In the *Odyssey*, hungry wanderers can win hospitality, respect, and food. With violence and with an inventive control of language, the Odyssean hero, against opposition, wins survival, homecoming, and reunion with his wife. Unlike Achilles, the hero of the *Iliad*, he need not choose between the pleasures of living and the requirements for fame; he wins both.

The *Odyssey* also allows for sympathetic representation of figures unheroic by Iliadic standards: women, slaves, the workers of the field and the household; and allows for a strong moralism. We are invited to judge unjust the disordered societies Odysseus encounters; we deem villainous the monsters who seek to eat or otherwise thwart the hero. At the same time, the *Odyssey* anticipates the most ambitious of later comedies in not keeping from us the complexities of its own conclusion: wife and husband are happily restored to one another, but the punishment of the enemies of their union pollutes their home. To restore order in his city, the hero must kill off its citizens.

A central concern of the Greek literary comedy in Athens of the 400s B.C.E., called Old Comedy, is likewise the pleasures of the belly and other bodily parts. The heroes of the comedies of Aristophanes (about 450 - 385 B.C.E.), with violence and with an inventive control of language, defy their limits: aging, death, political exclusion, and anything else that thwarts their pleasure. As the characters of Old Comedy are free from constraints, so is the genre's language and plot. Obscenity overturns the everday boundaries of dignified speech and the poet is freed from inherited myth to invent an original plot. The perspective of Old Comedy complements that of tragedy: if tragedy demands submission to the consequences of choice and implacable realities like death, comedy celebrates escape from these consequences and realities.

The comic festivals of Athens (and of many other places and times) incorporate into this literary comic myth the carnival themes of celebration of the grotesque and overturn of the everyday perhaps as an appropriate way of observing the time between the end of one season and beginning of the next. In liminal times, these times of transition, the usual order can be scrambled; the world is then put back together again in the right way. The hero comes back to life, the spring comes, we are glad for both; yet in the end our desire for an ordered year and ordered society cannot entirely be reconciled with our desire to see the comic hero succeed in overturning those orders. Athenian Old Comedy also claimed, however comically, an authority over the political and artistic forms of its city. Through parody, metatheater (the self-aware presentation of drama within drama), and even through direct addresses to the audience, it assumed the power to critique tragedy and political life. Comedy even called itself into question, never shy about making the audience notice the way it produced its illusion.

As the festival years went on and life in the Athenian city-state changed in the aftermath of the conquests of Alexander, Athenian comedy of the late fourth century B.C.E. becomes less interested in representing wild and fantastic extravagance and more interested in representing the lives of families and neighborhoods. If the hero of Old Comedy wanted the pleasures of peace and was blocked by villainous politicians, the young hero of this new style of comedy just wants to get drunk with his friends while his father's away, or to get married to the woman he loves in spite of her inappropriate social status and the grumpiness of his authoritarian father. For a plot that ends in the recovery of lost loves, comedy can now look to a group of tragedies with (not unambiguously) happy endings that Euripides staged in the late fifth century: *Helen, Iphigenia among the Taurians,* and *Ion.* In these plays, tragic disaster is averted and wife and husband, sister and brother, mother and son find one another and reconcile.

The new kind of Greek comedy is called New Comedy, and the most important practicioner known to us was Menander (about 342-290 B.C.E.). The famous remark of a Hellenistic scholar — "O Menander, o life, which one of you imitated the other?" — gives an indication of what this comedy tries to achieve. Like the *Odyssey,* Aristophanic comedy realistically acknowledges and dramatizes the unheroic needs and desires of the body, but is decidedly unrealistic in creating a fantasy world unchecked by logical consequence. Characters in New Comedy are more restrained in their language and in meeting community requirements. If the hero of Old Comedy can take sexual pleasure with impunity, the young lover of New Comedy must deal with the resulting pregnancy. He will escape the bitter consequences of his deed, but not by flying away: he will be forgiven or allowed to marry the now miraculously marriageable girl. As it becomes less concerned with the individual's defiance of communitarian responsiblities and restraints, New Comedy also loses the great choral song and dance numbers so prominent in Old Comedy. This Greek New Comedy is the comedy that in time interested and was adapted by the Romans.

Before they first encountered Greek literary culture, the Romans had their own traditions of comedy, and had also experienced, as their state expanded militarily, the dramatic forms of other Italian peoples. First, Rome had its own tradition of obscene, abusive poetry, performed at harvest time and weddings, the Fescennine verses. The Romans enjoyed the Oscans' comedy, unscripted slapstick called Atellan farce, performed by actors with masks, playing stock characters and situations, a distant origin, perhaps, of *commedia dell' arte.* The Romans also had a taste for Etruscan, especially musical, performance; the important Etruscan dramatic influence gives Latin two terms that survive to this day in our dramatic vocabulary: *histrio* "actor" and *persona* "mask".

After southern Italy, the area that was the western part of the Greek world, fell to the Romans in 270 B.C.E., the Romans began to have direct experience of the Greek New Comedy performed there and began to want to see versions of those plays in their own festivals. Scripted literary drama begins in Rome in 240 or so and the movement grows to translate Greek comedies into Latin and produce them. Most every Roman comedy is a translation of a Greek original. "Translation" is too restrictive word, however, for what the Roman comedians were doing, and undervalues the process by which they created original works of dramatic art. Plautus, the first Roman comedian whose works we have, called it *vortere*, 'turning': he translated, but also adapted, using the original as a jumping-off point for imaginative flights. He amplified the original with elements most congenial to Roman taste and his own: more clowning, more songs, more crude jokes. Because of this work of adaptation, the Roman experience of the same comic material had a detachment not characteristic of the Greek original, still a drama rooted in its own community. Roman comedy is set in Athens, yet precariously: its inhabitants speak Latin and make jokes about the decadence of those foreign Greeks. The city of Roman comedy is somewhere beween Athens and Rome, a fantasy nowhere, familiar enough for the Romans to enter into, far enough away to be dismissed if the comedy hits too close to home.

Roman theatrical production had always been open to foreign forms: Oscan, Etruscan, Greek. One among many great achievements of Plautus (who died in 184 B.C.E.), the great, foundational Roman comedian, is the integration of the native Italian dramatic traditions with the literary Athenian New Comedy. The comedies of Plautus result from an energetic mixture: they follow, broadly speaking, the structure and words of a Greek original, but also throw in duels of coarse abuse like Fescennine verses; characters more buffoonish than their Greek New Comedy counterparts reflecting Oscan *commedia*; and, most importantly, solo musical numbers, ever more as his career continued, popular with the Romans from Etruscan drama. In metatheatrical moments Plautus frequently boasts how his concoction far surpasses his sickly Greek model. By adding solo song to his version where it is lacking in the Greek original, Plautus adds an element distinctly Roman (or Etruscan) and at the same time restores to the comic tradition the musical element Aristophanes lost to Menander. By adding a native linguistic exuberance, he restores an appropriate comic excess edited out of Aristophanes by Menander.

Terence, successor to Plautus in the next generation of Roman comedians, reacted against many of the canons of Plautine art. Terence, as presumably did his patrons, preferred a finer Hellenism, a greater sensitivity to the subtleties of the Greek original, a "realer" Athens with fewer distractions, diction more refined, fewer buffoons, plots in which the scenes followed one another logically, characters true to life. To put it another way, Plautus characteristically chose to adapt more farcical Greek New Comedy models, while Terence chose to adapt models more restrained and neatly constructed. Terence avoids, rather than celebrates, the grotesque. This choice, at the expense of comic fantasy, allows him a greater degree of social realism. Plautine slaves joke elaborately about crucifixion and other tortures and as one outrageously preposterous lie is exposed they move boldly to the next. Terentian slaves, liable at all times to threats of casual violence, can, as at the beginning of *Phormio*, chat grimly about how difficult it is to keep their personal savings intact (their *peculia*, the money they will eventually use to buy their freedom) when their rich masters insist that the slaves buy them wedding presents. The slave of *The Eunuch* is realistically demoralized: living in a tiny uncomfortable cell, insufficiently fed, and susceptible to blackmail for eating the food his young master tempts him with.

A pledge of the literary ambition of Terence is the characteristic prickliness of his prologues. He is at pains to explain his procedures, his taste, and his expectations. While Terence does lack some of Plautus' ease in assembling an audience for the performance as people mill about the festival, when he defends himself in his prologues against literary enemies, he catches the attention of potential audience members by involving them in stories of behind-the-scenes intrigue and conspiracy. Terence's critics would charge him with "contaminating, spoiling" comic plots, bringing a scene from one Greek original into his version of another. *Contaminatio* is a technique available to a Roman comedian for handling his material creatively, but it used up the limited store of Greek plays, the possession of no one Roman comedian, twice as fast, to the detriment of all. Terence's *Brothers*, a version of Menander's *Brothers*, uses up another comedy as well, one by Diphilus, *Dying Together* (*Synapothneskontes*): *Brothers* adds the scene of a young man kidnapping a slave girl from a slave dealer, taken from *Dying Together*.

Plautus competes explicitly with his Greek models and boasts of his success. Terence is more subtle with his metatheater. The young husband at the end of *The Mother-in-law* (*Hecyra*), for example, decides the usual comic resolution of revelation, forgiveness, reconciliation is inadequate to his needs:

**Pamphilus**
    No need to tell my father.
I wouldn't like this to end up the way it does in comedies,
    where everybody finds out everything. Those who should have found
    out
    know already. Those who shouldn't know won't find out and won't
    know. (865-8)

He wants to keep his misbehavior suppressed, and plots the end of his comedy differently (as will, to catch an echo of the ancient comic tradition on the other side of 2160 years, two characters in Woody Allen's *Crimes and Misdemeanors* who discuss the plotting of the rest of their movie — should the murderer escape? — even as it ends with a wedding). Still, Terence and Plautus both inherit equally the comic responsibility to critique the civic and artistic forms of their city. Both acknowledge the Roman avidity for Greek culture; this occasions boasting, but also a metatheatrical anxiety: their own plays are prime examples of the importation of Greek culture.

How funny are Terence's comedies? The richness of the comic tradition in which Terence works suggests that this is not the only question to ask; the repetoire of comic characters, situations, and themes allows the comedian scope for both fantasy and the realistic privileging of those unprivileged in other genres. The richness comes in part from the contradictions implicit in the comic myth. On the one hand, comedy provides a mode for representing the overturn of hierarchy: Odysseus cheats death, the Aristophanic hero cheats the city, the young lover and slave of New Comedy can master the father. The comic hero escapes to win what he imagines. On the other hand, comedy can put right what has gone wrong: the wanderer returns, the lovers overcome opposition to their marriage, enemies are reconciled, the wrongly enslaved are set free. Comedy occasions both wild fantasy free of the boundaries of necessity and realistic representation of domestic situations and personal problems. It grants a temporary freedom to old men to be young and lecherous, to women to be politically powerful, to slaves to be masters; yet in its closure, which can be taken to be its moral view, it makes the old cede their places to the young, women return to their homes, slaves return to subservience. When ambitious comedies emphasize the complexities of their endings, we wonder if things really are being put back right in the end.

In Roman comedy this tension is particularly poignant for slaves. If we enjoy the festival inversion of their mastery over their masters, do we also accept their return to their places when festival and comedy are done? Plautus and Terence represent slaves and slave life with much greater elaboration than Greek comedy. This reflects the concerns of their audiences who faced the destabilizing consequences of slaveholding in ever larger numbers: periodic slave uprisings during the years the comedies were first performed and anxiety over the continued worth to the state of the labor of free citizens. Does Roman comedy console the anxieties of a slaveholding audience more than it frightens them with a vision of slaves empowered? Comedy can vary its outcome in many ways: the good slave is rewarded, the wicked slave is punished, the wicked slave is forgiven. Or alternatively, as in *Brothers*, the wicked slave is rewarded and the good slave is left in slavery.

When we experience ancient comedy, how do we balance the fun of the world upside down with a moral complicity in the way in which the world is put rightside up; the fun of a "happy" comic ending with the ironies of endings that offer forgiveness or justice or justice made ironic? The literary comedy of Terence recognizably preserves elements of the tradition from which it emerges, while it is far distanced from comedy's original celebration of the grotesque and the inverse. Terence is often bitterly funny, but remains comic even when not funny. We may be allowed to take Terence seriously.

## Production

Comedy in Rome in the time of Terence, the 160s B.C.E., was produced regularly (as was tragedy) as part of the celebration of annual religious festivals such as the *ludi Romani, ludi plebeii, ludi Apollinares*, and *ludi Megalenses*. Fifteen or so days a year called for dramatic performances, as did special occasions of honor such as military triumphs and distinguished funerals. *Brothers* was first produced in 160 B.C.E. for the funeral games honoring L. Aemilius Paulus, the victorious general of the battle of Pydna eight years before. Elected officials, *aediles* and *praetors*, had responsibility for putting on the games, and contracted for the performance of a play with the manager (*dominus gregis*) of a theatrical company (*grex*). The production notice to *Brothers* tells us that it was produced by the brothers P. Cornelius Scipio Aemilianus and Q. Fabius Maximus Aemilianus, the surviving sons of Aemilius. Roman actors were possibly members of a professional guild. The lead actors in the first performance of *Brothers*, again according to the production notice, were L. Hatilius and L. Ambivius Turpio, who was Terence's *dominus gregis*.

All citizens could attend these games at no charge and see the shows. Women attended. Slaves attended too, though they were not allowed a seat. Off from work, people came to these festivals with the expectation of a holiday's entertainment. At the same time, dramatic performance was conditioned by Roman religious life. The plays are an expression of community life and represent, superficially and deeply, community concerns before the assembled community. Because of this, when we read these plays we can see more than the playwright's simple desire to entertain and look as well to the ambition of the comedian who has as a traditional inheritance the capacity to represent the city to the city critically.

Success meant two different things to the Roman playwright: getting the play produced is one thing, grabbing and keeping the audience, which helped get the next play produced, is another. A Roman festival was like a fair: events and entertainments in parallel venues going on simultaneously. The play would have to compete with dancers, boxers, and gladiators as Terence found out to his sorrow. His prologues attest to his ambition, his need for a discerning audience, and his occasional failure, though Terence was a successful commercial playwright.

Terence's stage (*scaena, proscaena*) was temporary, built of wood on a field for the festival. We cannot imagine a huge stone Greek theater for the first performance of *Brothers*. The Romans were reluctant to commit to dramatic performance as a permanent part of Roman life. This prevented the building of permament stone theaters until a hundred years after Terence. Behind the stage, a building represented as many as three houses set along a street and the three front doors of the houses. Other entrances to the playing area were to the right and the left of the stage, representing, in our play, the way from downtown and the way from the country. The actors wore masks, wigs, and costumes, with traditional features that indicated character: male and female, young and old, slave and free.

Playing area implies dramaturgy; the Roman playing area called for dramaturgical adjustments to the adapted Greek drama conceived for a different theater. The Romans lose the dancing space, the *orchestra*, an element of the Greek theater between stage building and audience, and lose with it the chorus itself and the choral interludes of singing and dancing. The Roman audience is more physically immediate to the wooden Roman stage, and literary Roman comedy can more easily reflect the improvised fun of traditional unscripted comedy. The Roman audience is also faced more directly with house and door: in Roman comedy the house becomes an important symbol of moral order, and the door an important moral barrier. Greek dramas were performed without intermission, but Roman comedies for the most part were performed continuously, without even the punctuation of choral song (the fisherman chorus of Plautus' *Rope* is one exception), and without act division. (The divisions of Terence's plays into acts and scenes is a later editorial decision; they are not indicated in this translation.) If a choral interlude had covered a passage of time in a Greek original, the Roman comedian had to make adjustments. We have a striking example of this in *Brothers*: in Menander's version, choral performance could have covered the time it takes Demea to decide to undertake his wild change of heart. Here, Terence boldly (or awkwardly) refuses to make an adjustment and devises nothing to cover the moment between the end of a scene with Micio and Demea's renunciation of his old way of life.

All ancient drama, tragedy and comedy, Greek and Roman, was musical. Its audiences heard solo and choral songs, all accompanied by a double reed instrument, *aulos* in Greek, *tibia* in Latin. When we read and perform these plays, we need to remember that what remains of them is to some degree what we now call the libretto of an opera. Directors and actors of ancient drama sometimes put themselves in the untenable position of performing the lyric of an ancient song as if it were the text of a speech, instead of restoring the lyric's melody and somehow singing it. Parts of ancient dramas are the lyrics of songs whose melody has been lost, though not entirely; the rhythmical shape of the original melody is preserved in the quantitative meters of the original Greek or Latin words. Performers used basically two kinds of delivery in performing Roman comedy: speech (*diverbium*), in rhythms that approximate everyday speech, and song (*canticum*). The songs (*cantica*) are written in two kinds of rhythms: long lines whose rhythmical scheme can be repeated indefinitely and of which whole scenes can be constructed (patter songs in comic opera or rap songs may be comparable in some respects to this kind of Roman comic song) and shorter lines with varying rhythms, called polymetric (perhaps something like what we think of as lyric song). The kind of delivery used for a passage can be identified from the meter in which it is written. Song of both sorts was accompanied by the music of the reed player, the *tibicen*, the buzzing, piercing quality of whose music is a good accompaniment for singing out of doors. Speech was unaccompanied. To give some examples from our play, the opening of *Brothers*(prologue and first scene with Micio and Demea (1-154)), is performed in unaccompanied speech. *Tibia* music accompanies the singing of Aeschinus, Sannio, and Syrus (155-228) until it abruptly stops at line 228. The only polymetric song in the play belongs to Aeschinus (610-616). The reed player of the first performance of *Brothers* was Flaccus, slave of Claudius.

This translation of *Brothers* is in prose; it makes no attempt to reproduce in English verse the varieties of Latin verse. Instead, it identifies which delivery is implied by the meter of the Latin original, speech or song (and polymetric song), and indicates where the delivery changes. It is always interesting to ask why the playwright wrote a scene using one kind of delivery or another. Aeschinus sings a polymetric song, the only such song in *Brothers* and practically in all the rest of Terence — why just there? How does piping music and catchy rhythm heighten the scenes in which they occur? The extravagant language of Ctesipho as he enters praising his brother (254-260), and the grotesque elaboration of the violence that Geta would like to do to Aeschinus' family as he plays the traditional comic scene, always sung, of the messenger distracted by his haste (*servus currens*) (299-320), are more intelligible when we recognize that these passages are part of a patter song. What is the significance when the *tibia* accompaniment drops out in the middle of a scene?

Ancient plays come to us without stage directions. As we read the script, we must visualize the action that its words imply and think of the play as the totality of its script, its music, its performance. Ancient drama, performed as it was outside, in daylight, for a large audience, generally called attention in words to all the significant action. Entrances and exits are marked this way, as in "Here comes Ctesipho..." or "The door's opening...". The converse is also generally true: action not indicated by the words is not essential to the play. But it is always interesting to ask what the relation really is between the words and the stage action we imagine for the words. What do we need to imagine that is not indicated in the words? The most important evidence we have for stage directions, blocking, action, even the appropriate tone and production style, is the script itself. I have been parsimonious with stage directions to encourage readers to imagine the staging for themselves. I have deliberately avoided indications like "pensively" or "struts around," not only because they are unoriginal (or because the first thing actors do when they prepare a script is to cross such indications out) but especially because they prejudice judgements, such as whether a scene, a moment, or the whole play can best be communicated in an outrageous *commedia* style or in a restrained, realistic style.

## Terence's *Brothers*

Whatever the source in biography or social circumstance, the drama of Terence, with a relentless intelligence, delights in probing convenient hypocrisies and exposing limits in moral vision in the Roman society it directly and indirectly represents. The *Mother-in-Law (Hecyra)*, produced five years before *Brothers*, opens with the shop talk of two prostitutes who expertly distinguish love and marriage and conflate love and greed. This sets the tone in the prologue for a play in which a young husband berates the rapist of his wife before learning that it actually was he. In the lines quoted above, the young husband ends the play by dismissing the traditional comic denouement and deciding it is better to suppress the truth. In *The Eunuch* , produced the year before *Brothers*, a young lover beats up his slave eunuch to keep him quiet about the rape of a young prostitute, perpetrated by his brother disguised as the eunuch. He explains to the audience, "I couldn't see any other way of getting out of it without compromising my reputation." (715) While he contemplated taking the girl he lusted for, a mural painting of Zeus carrying off Ganymede inspired him. But if the morality of imitating wicked Greek models is made to seem dubious, is this adaptation of a Menander comedy suggesting to us that imitating Greek models is dubious? A slave poses another moral conundrum: is adultery actually possible in a whorehouse? While subject to a double standard regarding whores, the whore Thais expresses the most humane view of love in the play, whose erotic rivalries are resolved in a menage.

    *Brothers* shares the sharpness of these characteristic moments. The comedy explores the adequacy and inadequacy of a number of forms of social definition: can one give moral advice indifferently to one's own advantage? how best to keep one's slaves pacified? does the happy ending of a comedy falsify experience ? The most prominent tension in the play is, of course, the tension between the two older brothers. According to Demea, Micio is dangerously indulgent; according to Micio, Demea is mindlessly rigid. Micio's serene affability can be thought Epicurean; Demea's disciplined self-control can be thought Stoic. Their conflict reflects a contemporary Roman concern over the threat to traditional Roman education emphasizing law and physical endurance, posed by the new Greek education that emphasized philosophy, rhetoric, and art.

The father's worry that adolescent children will be corrupted by luxury is a typical tension in Roman comedy. Often it's the tricky slave making available corrupting pleasures to a son while the father is away on business. In the comic tradition the competition between two attitudes towards education ultimately reflects a scene in Aristophanes' *Clouds*. There, two schools of thought, one traditional and rigorous, the other innovative and self-indulgent, vie for the chance to educate an impressionable student. Critics and audiences try to evaluate which is the more sinister — Micio's city bachelorhood, permissiveness, and desire to be his son's friend, or Demea's country family life, hardness, and desire to teach his son discipline. Actors and directors in particular productions can make choices and commit themselves to one interpretation or another, but the Terentian avoidance of the broader aspects of his predecessor Plautus suggests that we should hesitate to treat these characters as comic stereotypes.

*Brothers*, as comedy can, varies all its traditional elements in a realistic and individualizing way and complicates our responses to a number of stock situations. The dealer in young slave women (*leno*) is a stereotypically evil, vicious character in comedy. Yet in *Brothers*, Sannio suffers beating and theft unjustly and is the only character capable of viewing the seamier transactions of the household with honesty. He can articulate the double standard to which he is subject: citizens will buy slaves from him, yet hold him in contempt and deny him legal recourse because he sells slaves. Syrus is a tricky slave, but his trickiness consists not so much in vertiginous fiction as in subtle, intelligent negotiation to fix quietly a family scandal that needs fixing.

Aeschinus has done a stereotypical thing — while drunk he has raped and impregnated the girl next door — but this is viewed in several ways by several characters. Geta, the slave of the girl's family, repeats that it was a rape, brutal and violent. To Hegio it's understandable and excusable: "He was overwhelmed: night, desire, wine, he's a young man. It's human nature." (470-1) Aeschinus' immediate confession to her family and pledge to marry her and his tortured remorse and the hopeless love he expresses when he thinks he has lost her by his delay modify the picture. But if we think that Geta is simply being grumpy about a true romance, we never see the girl or hear her, except for her screams of pain in labor, while

Demea emphasizes the physical difficulty she will have, just having given birth, in completing the ritual movement of the ancient wedding, the procession to the house of her husband (*deductio in domum mariti*). In the ancient city, the question of whether Aeschinus and Pamphila were lovers consensually has little meaning. Sexual activity between young citizens unsupervised by the family and the city could only be illicit because it threatened to destabilize the legitimate inheritance of property.

As the play complicates these situations, so it would have us avoid easy choices about the fathers. *Brothers* dramatizes not the conflict of two schools of thought so much as the conflict of two individuals. To argue the merits of the Just education or the Unjust education in *Clouds* is futile: Aristophanes presents both systems as grotesque parodies. *Brothers* presents the two positions of the older brothers as at least partially plausible attitudes: those raising children can dispense entirely with neither nurture nor discipline. Neither brother attempts a fully argued, cogent philosophical defense. Both of them think at a level of popular morality and philosophy. As comedy does, the play represents the haphazard process by which people, making as much sense of their lives as they can while they live them, try to apply abstract moral principles to everday circumstances.

The question of staging is always crucial to interpretation. Asking 'why does Aeschinus sing a song?' can take us to the center of the play's concerns. Aeschinus, young lover in distress, sings a brief polymetric *canticum* before the house of his beloved (610-616). Terence in general declined to write for his comedies the solo polymetric songs so characteristic of Plautus. This is virtually the only polymetric *canticum* in Terence. Why here? Outwardly this song looks like a *paraclausithyron*, the song sung by a miserable young lover at the door of his lover's house, lamenting the barrier that excludes him from her. Yet this lover confuses the form: his torture comes not from his exclusion from the girl, but from having kept the secret from his father, a father who takes such pride in his son's openness with him. Singing this *canticum* gives Aeschinus a moment of intense introspection unique in Terence that goes some way to vindicate the style of Micio's education. The permissive villain has successfully taught his son to feel a tortured (if tardy) responsibility for his actions; the son of the disciplinarian has not learned to take responsibility for his own love affair.

If Aeschinus' song is an important innovation by Terence that tends to vindicate Micio, the largest structural innovation, the adding of the abduction scene to *Brothers* from another play, tends to undermine Micio. After his lengthy moralizing about his successful child-rearing with which the play opens, we cut immediately to see Aeschinus at his most uncontrolled. Doing and threatening violence, though out of his depth with the experienced slave dealer, and acting not for his own selfish pleasure but out of love for his brother, Aeschinus has kept this expedition as another secret from his father. The addition of this violent action from another play has its entertainment value, but it is not meant simply to satisfy the lower appetites of the audience. It further complicates our response to the relation of father to son and brother to brother.

Terence is famously sententious; the *sententiae* are made ironic when we see them in context. "I am a human being: nothing human is foreign to me" (*Heauton Timoroumenos* 77) is the most famous remark in Terence, but it is less a call to ecumenical brotherhood than a defense of being a nosy neighbor. The value of moral advice is problematic also in *Brothers*. The play opens with Micio's witty observation, "It's better to experience what your wife suspects than what a parent fears...," but we soon find out that bachelor Micio has no personal reason to know this. Hegio is the most relentless moralizer in the play, yet his authority as pillar of the community who always "shoulders his responsibilities" is compromised by his tardy involvement in Sostrata's family problem, Demea's declaration that the fatherless family has no one take care of them, and our sense that a slave is really the family's mainstay, not to mention the overlength of his advice. His pious judgement, "Aeschinus, you have not taken after your father" (450) is ridiculously inadequate to a son with two fathers. Demea tosses back in Micio's face his brother's pious saying, "Friends hold all in common," uttered now in cynical revenge, not generosity, and yet not less valid for the inadequacy of its quotation. Is virtue ever entirely devoid of self-interest? The Terentian truism is often false.

The truism that comedies end happily with the union of lovers and the reconciliation of the unreconciled likewise rings false in *Brothers*. Superficially all the comic resolutions are achieved: son is reconciled with father, brother is reconciled with brother, the treachery imputed to the young lover is revealed as a mistake, the perspectives of both feuding brothers are acknowledged, two slaves are manumitted, the faithful support of Hegio is rewarded when his poverty is eased. If a comedy ends with a wedding, *Brothers* obliges with an overabundance: Aeschinus marries Pamphila; Micio will marry Sostrata; Syrus can now legitimately marry Phrygia; and Ctesipho gets to keep Bacchis, the music-girl he loves.

Demea, who manages to bring so much of it about as a destructive practical joke to vindicate himself, falsifies the festivity. If we admired his strength of character, we're surprised to see him suddenly as a petulant spendthrift. If we condemn him for reversing his restraint, we can still view it as a pathetic attempt to win the respect and affection to which he is entitled as a dutiful father. So does the play deny us the pleasure of an easy, satisfying ending. If we're happy to discover that biological father and son, Demea and Aeschinus, are like one another after all, we're disconcerted to see that their similarity lies in a propensity for bashing down proper boundaries.

A concern for barriers breached is thematic in *Brothers*. Demea figures the delinquency of Aeschinus in the door he breaks down to abduct the girl for his brother, "He broke down a door and forced his way into a stranger's house..." (88-89) Yet to facilitate the wedding of Pamphila to his son, Demea himself is ready to urge Aeschinus to break down the wall separating Micio's house from Sostrata's (a boundary between houses that has, in a way, already been breached by the premarital pregnancy):

> Forget all that,
> the wedding hymn, the crowds, the torches, the reed players.
> Just have the garden wall between your two houses
> knocked down, immediately. Bring her into your house that way.
> Make one house of the two. Bring to our house her mother
> and all her family. (906-910)

For Demea to suggest the rupturing of ritual structure is more destructive than to suggest the rupture of the garden wall: in the ancient city, the ritual, legal, and social features of marriage were all interconnected. "A wedding without torches" was proverbial in Greek for illigitimacy; torches were metonymic for the whole of a Roman wedding. For Aeschinus to accept Demea's counsel, and proceed without the torches and forego a procession through the street (*pompa*) as public declaration of his marriage, is to undermine its legitimacy (an ambiguity famously exploited by Vergil in the *Aeneid*, for example, when lightning serves as the torch and the sky as a witness to the union of Aeneas and Dido).

Physical barriers of door and fence, and ritual barriers that regulate human life, are at issue in *Brothers*, as are the proper boundaries of family relationships, the concern that so troubles the plots of Athenian tragedy. Aeschinus in the joy of his father's forgiveness articulates a deeply important question of boundaries: "Is this to be a father or is this to be a son? If he were my brother or my friend, could he have done more perfectly what I wanted him to do?" (707-8) The relationship of father to son threatens to disintegrate and become that of brother to brother or friend to friend. This confusion resonates with the play's most prominent conflict: is disciplined governance (*imperium*) or friendship (*amicitia*) the proper model for the relationship of father to son?

In offering his son friendship, Micio brings to confusion the uniquely Roman paternal authority a Roman father held over the lives in his household, the patria potestas. While Aeschinus sings his song at the door, a proper boundary, a symbol of parental supervision over those who live behind it, he is anxious not for his girl, but about his father, thereby confusing its form. The father soon appears in the doorway, an image of the paternal authority the door symbolizes, but the scene that follows flirts further with Aeschinus' confusion between lover and father:

**Aeschinus**
May the gods curse me if I don't love you more than my own eyes!
**Micio**
What? more than her?
**Aeschinus**
Well, just as much. (701-2)

In the absence of his mother, the son must leave his father in order to marry a wife.

Can father (*pater*) be friend (*amicus*)? The play does not answer this simply. Indulgence has not ruined responsibility in Aeschinus, yet friendship threatens to abolish his father's authority. Aeschinus does prove spoiled at play's end, begging Micio for more and more money, yet only at the instigation of his biological father, famous for his frugality. The old brothers are alienated as they represent two sides of an ultimately unresolveable polarity. Ctesipho praises his brother for kidnapping the slave girl he loves in much the same terms that Aeschinus praises his father for arranging his marriage to the citizen he loves. The young brothers are linked with inappropriate closeness as one involves the other in pandering and assault. To what does the title *Brothers* actually refer: the older brothers, the younger brothers, or brotherhood as a dubiously appropriate model for father and sons?

The festive manumission of Syrus disturbs the happiness of the play's ending as much as the vindictiveness of Demea and his careless attitude toward ritual observance. The Romans regularly freed their slaves as a reward for good service (*fides*), as an incentive for them to behave and live long enough to see the day of freedom. As *Brothers* ends, the impudent trickster slave along with his slave wife is given freedom as his reward, while the faithfully servile, obedient slave Geta looks on. Not only that, but Demea delivers a parody of this element of the ideology of Roman slaveholding:

> I vote that Syrus be made a free man...
> buying party supplies on credit, procuring them prostitutes,
> preparing dinners in broad daylight:
> These are the duties of a distinguished man...
> And finally, today, he was the facilitator
> in buying that music girl. He got the job done.
> It's the right thing that he profit from it.
> The other slaves will be the better for it. (959-969)

Overtly, *Brothers* ends with generosity and forgiveness. Almost as overtly, the generosity proves a cynical stunt, the wedding ritual proves corrupted, the manumission proves a joke. *Brothers* causes us to question the applicability of the ways in which we represent the world to ourselves:

the way we frame moral questions, the way we theorize about raising children, the way we justify slaveholding to ourselves, the way we figure our lives in artistic forms such as the conventional behavior of young lovers and the conventions of comedy .

To catch another echo of the ancient comic tradition, *Brothers* ends similarly to an episode of *The Simpsons* (3G03) on Fox Television, another comedy relentlessly concerned with the validity of musical forms. The *matrona* of the household, losing her blue hair from stress, wants to hire a nanny. Shary Bobbins gets the job. This presents an opportunity for a close parody of the plot and musical numbers of the Disney movie of the P.L. Travers novel *Mary Poppins*. The magical visitor cannot, however, save the slovenly Simpsons who end the episode celebrating their grotesque faults with a chorus, "We're happy with things the way they are." The nasty parody suggests the inadequacy of Victorian myth and the conventions of musical comedy as a model for family life in the late 20th century. At the same time, the ending cannot endorse the complacent self-assertion of moronic buffoons.

The ending of *Brothers* is similarly unstable; comedy as a genre can examine social forms, while the comic ending offers a false comfort. Children need discipline, but also nurture, in a situation particularly precarious because in this family the children lack their mother and her mediation. Moral instruction functions with perfect validity only when it intersects perfectly with self-interest. Slaveholding is more palatable when the service of faithful slaves is believed regularly rewarded by eventual manumission, except when it pleases a bitter man to make mock of that strategy. *Brothers* defies us to reconcile social contradictions: permissiveness and rigidity, virtue and selfishness, festivity and social order. In doing so it has represented the world comically in the deepest sense: moral judgements are uncertain because they are made necessary by the unheroic, compromised needs of everyday life.

## Suggestions for Further Reading

Editions of the Latin text of *Adelphoe* with commentary are R. H. Martin (Cambridge 1976), and A. S. Gratwick (Aris and Philips 1987) with translation.

On performance and context see the relevant sections of Eric Csapo and William J. Slater, *The Context of Ancient Drama* (Michigan 1995); R. C. Beacham, *The Roman Theater and its Audience* (Harvard 1992), which discusses reconstruction of the stage at the time of Terence; E. Rawson, "Theatrical Life in Republican Rome and Italy" *Papers of the British School at Rome* 53 (1985) 97-113; C. Garton *Personal Aspects of the Roman Theater* (Toronto 1972); George E. Duckworth, *The Nature of Roman Comedy*

(Princeton 1952).

Some general books: D.F. Sutton, *Ancient Comedy* (1993); Sander M. Goldberg, *Understanding Terence* (Princeton 1986); W.E. Forehand, *Terence* (Twayne's 1985); R.L. Hunter, *The New Comedy of Greece and Rome* (1985); and F.H. Sandbach, *The Comic Theater of Greece and Rome* (1978).

For background on Roman society see on slavery, Keith Bradley, *Slavery and Society at Rome* (Cambridge 1994); on marriage, Susan Treggiari, *Roman Marriage* (Oxford 1991); on the settling of legal disputes in New Comedy, Adele C. Scafuro, *The Forensic Stage* (Cambridge 1997); on brotherhood, Cynthia J. Bannon, *The Brothers of Romulus* (Princeton 1997); on friendship, David Konstan, *Friendship in the Classical World* (Cambridge 1997).

Articles on *Brothers*: David W. Frauenfelder, "Respecting Terence, *Adelphoe* 155-75" in *Classical World* 90 (1996); Sander Goldberg, "Terence's *Adelphoe* on Stage" in *Classical Outlook*, May-June 1986; N.A. Greenberg, "Success and Failure in *Adelphoe*" in *Classical World* 73 (1979); C. Lord, "Aristotle, Menander, and the *Adelphoe* of Terence" in *TAPA* 107 (1977); J.N. Grant, "The Ending of Terence's *Adelphoe* and the Menandrian Original" in *AJP* 96 (1975); W.R. Johnson, "Micio and the Perils of Perfection" in *CSCA* 1 (1968).

## A video production of Terence's *Brothers*

In the spirit of filmmakers like John Waters and Robert Rodriguez, who allowed neither underfinancing nor inexperience to preclude a first feature, Alexander Gombach and I undertook a production partnership, The Terence Project, to make a low-budget film of the script of *Brothers*. That script has become the book published here with some changes, and the video of it is also available from Focus.

*Brothers* by Terence was shot, for economy, in Beta video format on the campus of Vassar College in August, 1995. Production requires choices; for those who watch the video in conjunction with reading this translation, I here highlight some choices we made and, for the sake of aiding discussion, pose some of the implications of those choices.

The production treated the piece more as a realistic evocation of life in the ancient city than as a rambunctious comedy: it was set outdoors, somewhat realistically (using two brick houses that were once the Creamery of the Vassar farm); it often showed the faces of unmasked actors in closeup; the actors built individual characters rather than indicated stereotypes. Conveying the painful situation of an ancient mother without a husband whose daughter has been raped and made pregnant, or something of what life was like for slaves in a household, was more important than trying to get laughs. Can a sense of the realities of ancient life legitimately be sought from Roman comedy? Does this production style distort

Terentian drama?  Should the production have tried to be more funny? Does this production style make unintelligible a traditional comic routine, like that of the slave distracted by his haste (*servus currens*) (Geta, 299-322)? To convey the rhythm and musicality of long canticum lines is almost impossible in translation, thus the choice simply to speak them as prose. What is lost by performing in speech such musical scenes as the extravagant praise by Ctesipho of his brother (254-9), or Demea's reversal of mind (855-81)?  To emphasize the unusualness of Aeschinus' polymetric song, the production gives him a song to sing (610-617), but, without the context of other music, it seems out of place. How can a musical play come across in translation with no music?  How could background music be used, as analogy to the musical structure of the original?  This was something the production, without adequate resources for sound mixing, could not attempt.

Many videos of ancient drama record stage productions without using the language of film, which involves the juxtaposition of images, cutting. Many films of ancient drama are a director's version of a myth rather than a direction of the ancient author's version of a myth. This production sought both a fidelity to the text and an adaptation in film.  If it is true that film communicates not so much through what happens within a shot as in the cutting from one shot to another, film is not a good medium for the representation of conversation. Whether ancient drama can be made into film at all becomes debatable. Some examples from the production of how editing—cutting between images—imposes an interpretation on a scene are: intercutting in various rhythms between the faces of Syrus and Sannio to underline the ebb and flow of delicate negotiations (209-253), cutting to the faces of Pamphila and Canthara for reactions to Demea's praise of Syrus for providing Aeschinus with prostitutes (965), cutting to the face of the faithful Geta for Demea's "...the slaves will be the better for it..." (968), cutting to the faces of other slaves while Syrus is manumitted (970). If the cut from sullen Demea to converted Demea (854-855) is awkward in stage performance, it works nicely cinematically; the story is told in the cut to a face now adorned with a wreath.

Are the monologues (like Micio's 55 line monologue with which the piece opens) playable in film?  What is the effect of shooting them into the camera or away from the camera?  Are we as open to ancient characters talking about themselves straight to the camera as we are to the Brooklynites doing the same in Spike Lee's *She's Gotta Have It*?

The film shows two actions not a part of the play in its original staging: the tearing down of the wall and a final wedding celebration. We see images of the ancient wedding: the bride's veil, the groom's hand on her wrist, a procession of sorts through the torn-down wall, the pouring down of grain for good luck, dancing, music. As a consequence of this choice, we must see Pamphila herself, whom Terence did not show us. By asking questions not asked in the original production, how successfully does this additional material highlight some of the anomalies of the play's ending? How does Pamphila feel about the wedding? How do slaves react to the manumission of a fellow slave when not manumitted themselves? How moralizing is the ending as performed here?

How do the choices of the actors in the film affect our take on questions perennially asked of the piece: is Micio sympathetic or sinister? is Demea inconsistent or calculating? Do we answer these questions differently in reaction to performance and reading? For a contemporary audience, does a broader question such as what is the play's attitude toward slavery emerge more naturally from watching a video or from reading the words?

*A Funny Thing Happened the Way to the Forum* is inevitably what people think of when they think of Roman comedy in performance. Can productions of Roman comedy achieve more than festive silliness? Gelbart, Shevelove, and Sondheim, the creators of *Funny Thing*, stand in the same creative relation to Plautus as Plautus and Terence stand in to Diphilus and Menander; Plautine comedy is really about Rome, not Athens, and *Funny Thing* is really about '60s America, not Rome. Can productions of Roman comedy really take us into the Roman society of 2200 years ago?

# THE ANCIENT PRODUCTION NOTICE

HERE BEGINS ADELPHOE (BROTHERS) BY TERENCE. THE GREEK PLAY THAT TERENCE TRANSLATES AND ADAPTS IS ADELPHOE BY MENANDER. IT WAS PRODUCED AT THE FUNERAL GAMES FOR L. AEMILIUS PAULUS WHICH WERE PUT ON BY Q. FABIUS MAXIMUS AND P. CORNELIUS SCIPIO AEMILIANUS AFRICANUS. THE PRINCIPAL ACTORS WERE L. HATILIUS FROM PRAENESTE AND L. AMBIVIUS TURPIO. FLACCUS, SLAVE OF CLAUDIUS, PLAYED THE ACCOMPANIMENT ON THE TYRIAN DOUBLE-REEDS THROUGHOUT THE PRODUCTION. THIS WAS TERENCE'S SIXTH PRODUCTION, PRODUCED IN THE CONSULSHIP OF M. CORNELIUS CETHEGUS AND L. ANICIUS GALLUS (160 BCE).

# B|TERENCE BROTHERS

## (*Adelphoe*)

## CHARACTERS

**Micio** (*senex*) is 64, elegant, luxurious, somewhat careless of responsibility. Remarkably for his culture, he is unmarried; he is well-off, has a beautiful city house, and likes his solitary pleasure. He has adopted his brother's teenage son, Aeschinus, some years ago, and has raised him permissively and progressively. Micio has a sententious wit and likes to lecture others, but the action of the piece tests his theories of living.

**Demea** (*senex*) is Micio's brother, tough, frugal, grouchy, espouser of traditional values of thrift, a dweller in the country on his farm. He is a widower and has two sons, the older of which, Aeschinus, he let Micio adopt. Demea is a pain in everyone's neck, but, in his own mind at least, represents old-fashioned virtue and the responsible child-rearing without which sons are spoiled and corrupted. Micio and Demea clash over this issue.

**Aeschinus** (*adulescens*) is the son of Demea adopted by Micio, a teenager, the young lover of the girl next door. He has taken advantage of Micio's permissiveness, but has not lost all of Demea's rigorous sense of responsibilty.

**Ctesipho** (*adulescens*) is the son of Demea, raised by him on the farm. Another pubescent young lover, he is in love with the slave girl his brother eventually arranges to buy. He adores his older brother, who

21

has opened up for him cultivated city life. Torn about his behavior, he finds it difficult to disobey his father.

**Syrus** (*servus*), an older man, senior slave in Micio's household, a tricky slave. Syrus is impudent, sarcastic, an accomplished liar; his deviousness serves his masters well, to whose interests he proves devoted. He is the fixer, the one who successfully drives a hard bargain with a slave dealer.

**Dromo** (*puer*), slave in Micio's household, a cook.

**Parmeno** (*servus*), slave in Micio's household.

**Sannio** (*leno*), middle-aged man, the nasty, disreputable dealer in slaves, especially young women. He provides a service that is availed of, but is under no illusions about his trade or the contempt in which he is nevertheless held. He is just trying to make a living.

**Sostrata** (*matrona*), an older widow with an unmarried daughter, who lives next door to Micio. She is poor and devoted to the honor and dignity of her family. Her daughter's pregnancy causes her much grief, but is just the challenge to bring out her toughness.

**Pamphila** (*virgo*), Sostrata's daughter, the girl next door, raped and made pregnant by Aeschinus.

**Geta** (*servus*), an older man, the dutiful senior slave of Sostrata's household. He is serious about doing all he can to uphold the family of Sostrata.

**Canthara** (*anus*), old woman, nurse, slave of Sostrata's family.

**Hegio** (*senex*), an older man, a pillar of the community, though of less property than Micio, a serious man who agreed to look out for the family of Sostrata when his friend, her husband, died. He takes this commitment as a sacred obligation.

**Bacchis** (*meretrix*), young woman, the prostitute-slave loved and bought by Ctesipho.

**PROLOGUE** *(Delivery is unaccompanied speech)*
When the playwright realized that his work
was being attacked unfairly and that his enemies
were doing violence to the play we are about to act,
he wanted to submit to trial: *you* will be the judges
whether his work should be praised or blamed.
*Synapothneskontes* is a comedy by Diphilus.
Plautus adapted it as the play *Dying Together*.                    10
In the original Greek, near the beginning, there is a young man
who kidnaps a prostitute from a slave dealer.
Plautus left that scene out entirely, so Terence
translated it word for word and used it in *Brothers*.
We are about to act the play for the first time.
Judge carefully whether you think he stole
or actually rescued a scene that was carelessly cut out.
As for what those evil-minded men are saying,
"he gets help from important Romans,
they practically write his plays for him"
—what they think is a nasty insult he thinks is the highest praise:
he wins the approval of those who win
the approval of all of you, the whole city.
Each one of you in time of need has relied upon
their generous service in war, in peace, in industry.            20
Now don't expect a plot summary.
The two old men who will appear first
will explain the story in part
and the rest will be made clear as the action unfolds.
Make sure your fairness encourages the playwright
to work even harder writing plays!

*(Two houses on a street in a city imagined to be Athens. One, the more*
*opulent, is Micio's; the other, the more humble, is Sostrata's. Two entrances*
*on either side, one from the town, the other from the country.)*

*(Micio enters from his house.)*

## MICIO

*(calling a slave)*
Storax!
Aeschinus never got back last night from his party.
None of the slaves who went to get him either.
Well, I'm sure what they say is true:
if you're gone for awhile, or off on your own,
it's better to have happen to you what your wife accuses you of            30

or what she thinks in her heart when she's mad
than what loving parents fear.
Your wife, if you're gone for a while, thinks you're having an affair
or you're out gambling
or you're out drinking and having a good time
off by yourself while she's alone and miserable.
But my son is gone and I know what I'm afraid of.
I'm worried. I hope he's not cold.
I hope he hasn't had an accident. I hope he hasn't broken a bone or
 something.
Why in the world should a man take it in to his head
to make something for himself that is dearer to him
than his own life? He's not my son by birth, you know,                40
but my brother's. Ever since we were children
my brother and I have been totally different.
I've led a charming life here in the city. I like my leisure.
And, what my friends tell me is a blessing, I never married.
My brother's been exactly the opposite.
He lives in the country. Tough. Frugal. He married, had two sons.
I adopted the elder of the two,
and I've brought him up since he was a boy.
I have held him, and loved him, as my own.
He's my greatest joy, the one thing I love.
And I do my best that he should feel the same way about me.        50
I give him money. I let him do what he wants.
I don't think it necessary to exercise my full parental authority.
In fact, other boys keep what they do secret from their fathers
—you know how boys are. But I have trained my son
not to hide anything from me.
If a boy gets used to lying and deceiving his father,
he'll be more likely to lie and deceive others.
I believe that respect and freedom is a better discipline
for freeborn sons than fear.
My brother and I disagree on this, and he's not happy about it.
He's always coming to me and yelling at me,                        60
"What are you doing, Micio?
What's he having these love affairs for?
What's he drinking for? What are you ruining our boy for?
Why are you racking up our bills for all this?
You buy him too many clothes! You're a terrible father!"
He's much too harsh, beyond what's the right thing
and the proper thing.
If you want to know my opinion,

it's a terrible mistake to think that authority based on force
has more weight and stability
than authority that's joined by friendship.
My theory is this, my philosophy of bringing up children is this:
when you use punishment to force your child to obey you,
he worries only about not getting caught.                              70
If he thinks he can get away with something,
he reverts right back to his natural state.
But when you join your son to you in kindness,
he acts sincerely, he is eager to treat you the same way.
Whether he's with you or far away from you, he behaves the same.
That's a real father: training his son
to do what's right on his own,
not out of fear of anyone else.
That's the difference between a father and a slave-owner.
A man who doesn't know the difference
between a father and a slave-owner
should admit he has no idea how to rule his freeborn sons.
*(Demea enters from the country.)*
Well, is this the very man I was talking about?
It is the man I was talking about.
I see he's rather angry.
I suppose it's time for his usual abuse.                               80

You're looking very well, Demea.

**DEMEA**
Well that's just fine. I've been looking for you.

**MICIO**
What's wrong?

**DEMEA**
You're asking me what's wrong.
We've got an Aeschinus on our hands
and you're asking me what's wrong.

**MICIO**
*(aside)* Didn't I tell you?
What's he done?

**DEMEA**
What's he done? A boy who's ashamed of nothing,
who's afraid of no one,
who thinks no law restrains him?

I won't mention what's gone on in the past.
Do you want to know his latest outrage?

**MICIO**

What is it?

**DEMEA**

He broke down a door
and forced his way into a stranger's house.
He beat up the owner and the whole household
almost to death. He abducted a woman he's in love with.          90
It's a disgrace. Everyone's talking about it.
Everyone I run into tells me about it, Micio.
It's on everybody's lips.
I tell you, if he needs an example
why can't he look to his brother, frugal and sober,
who pays attention to his work on the farm?
These two brothers aren't alike at all.
And when I reproach him, Micio, I reproach you:
you've allowed him to be corrupted.

**MICIO**

There's nothing more unjust
than a man without experience of the world;
he thinks nothing right but what he's done himself.

**DEMEA**

And what's that supposed to mean?          100

**MICIO**

That you're misjudging this.
It's not a crime, believe me, for a boy
to fool around a little bit with prostitutes,
to go drinking. It's not.
And breaking down a door isn't a crime either.
If you and I never fooled around, it's because we couldn't afford it.
Now you're taking credit for how we behaved
when we just didn't have the money to do anything else?
It's not right. If we had had the opportunity,
we would have done the same thing.
If you were at all a human being,
you'd let that son of yours do this sort of thing now,
while he's young, rather than later,
when at long last he's tossed your corpse out of the house
and behaves that way at a less appropriate age.          110

**DEMEA**
Well, Juppiter! You're the man to drive me insane.
It's not a crime for a boy to do all this?

**MICIO**
Oh, pay attention to me, will you, so you stop
banging my ear again and again and again on this.
You gave me your son to adopt. He's become mine.
If he commits an offense, Demea, he commits it on my behalf.
I will take responsiblity.
He goes to parties, he drinks, he perfumes himself: it's on me.
He's in love, he'll have money from me
as long as it's within reason.
And when it isn't, perhaps then she'll close the door on him.
So he broke down a door; I'll send a carpenter.                    120
He tore up someone's clothes in a fight; I'll send a tailor.
I have — thank the gods — I have the means to do this,
and so far, it hasn't been a problem.
So, finally, either shut up
or let someone appoint us an arbitrator.
I will prove that you are the one who's at fault, not I.

**DEMEA**
Listen to me, learn how to be a father
from one who really knows.

**MICIO**
You are his father by nature;
I am his father in the way I brought him up.

**DEMEA**
You, in the way you brought him up?

**MICIO**
Ah, if you're going to go on, I'm leaving —

**DEMEA**
So this is how you're treating me?

**MICIO**
And I'm supposed to listen to the same thing
over and over and over...

**DEMEA**
Well, I'm concerned.

**MICIO**
Well, I'm concerned too. But really, Demea,
why don't we split the concern:                                    130
you take care of your son and I'll take care of mine.

If you're going to try to take care of both,
you might as well demand back the son you gave me to adopt.

**DEMEA**

Ah, Micio...

**MICIO**

Well that's the way I see it.

**DEMEA**

All right, then. If that's what you want,
let him squander, waste, and be wasted.
What do I care? But if after this I hear one word...

**MICIO**

Getting angry again, Demea?

**DEMEA**

Don't you believe me?
Am I asking for the son I gave you back?
It's sickening. I'm his father.
But if I oppose — oh, all right.
You want me to take care of mine,
I'll take care of mine, and — thank the gods —
he's the kind of son I want.
That son of yours will understand one day.
I won't say anything worse about him.                          140

*(Demea exits to the town.)*

**MICIO**

There's something to what he says,
but he's not entirely right.
Even if this business is a bit out of hand,
I wasn't going to let him know that I was worried.
He's the sort of man that when I want to calm him down
I've got to fight him and scare him off.
Even then he scarcely behaves like a human being.
If I really got him angry or responded to it
I'd immediately become as insane as he is.
It's true Aeschinus has to some degree
offended me in this matter.
What prostitute has he not fallen in love with?
What slave dealer has he not had to pay off?              150
Bored with it all, I guess,
he finally started talking about getting married.
I was hoping his adolescence had cooled down,
and I was pleased. And now look, all over again!

Well, I would like to know exactly what happened
and meet this man. I'll find him in the forum.

*(Micio exits to the town.)*
*(Aeschinus and Parmeno enter from town together leading Bacchis. Sannio
pursues. Delivery changes from unaccompanied speech to **canticum**.)*

**SANNIO**
Help! Help me! I beg you people,
save a wronged and innocent man.
Help me! I need help!

**AESCHINUS**
*(to the girl)*
Easy. Stop right here. Don't look back.
There's no danger. As long as I'm here,
he'll never touch you.

**SANNIO**
I'll get her all right.

**AESCHINUS**
As dirty a criminal as he is,
he won't make the mistake
of getting beaten up twice.

**SANNIO**
Aeschinus, listen to me.                                    160
It's not as if you can say
you didn't know what kind of man I am.
I'm a sex-slave dealer.

**AESCHINUS**
I know that.

**SANNIO**
But as honest a slave dealer as ever there was.
And as for excusing yourself later,
"I really didn't mean to hurt you,"
you can forget it. Believe me, I'll get my rights in court.
You won't be paying off in words
what you did to me in deeds.
I know the sort of thing you boys say,
"I didn't mean to do it. I'll swear an oath.
You got hurt, but it was unintentional."
Well, I don't deserve this treatment.

**AESCHINUS**
Hurry up, open the door.

**SANNIO**
So you're going to ignore me?

**AESCHINUS**
Get inside now.

**SANNIO**
And I won't allow it.

*(Scuffle for the girl.)*

**AESCHINUS**
Here, get in front of him, Parmeno.

Yes, that's right. Now don't take your eyes off mine.                    170
If I give the signal, you instantly punch him in the chin.

**SANNIO**
I'd like to see him try.

**AESCHINUS**
Look out! Let go of the girl.

*(Scuffle. Parmeno punches Sannio.)*

**SANNIO**
It's an outrage! An outrage!

**AESCHINUS**
He'll do it again if you're not careful.

*(Parmeno again hurts Sannio.)*

**SANNIO**
Oh. oh...

**AESCHINUS**
I hadn't given the signal, but true enough,
better to err on the side of violence. Now get inside.

*(Parmeno and Bacchis go into Micio's house.)*

**SANNIO**
So what is this? This is your kingdom, is it?

**AESCHINUS**
If I were the king you would be rewarded
according to what you deserve.

**SANNIO**
What business do you have with me?

**AESCHINUS**
Nothing.

**SANNIO**
Do you know the kind of man I am?

**AESCHINUS**
I have no desire for that kind of knowledge.

**SANNIO**
Have I touched anything of yours?

**AESCHINUS**
If you had, you'd be suffering for it.

**SANNIO**
What greater right do you have
to possess my girl, whom I paid for? Tell me.

**AESCHINUS**
It's better for you not to make a scene here                 180
in front of the house. If you continue to bother me
you'll be taken inside and worked over
with the whip until you're dead.

**SANNIO**
A whipping for a free man?

**AESCHINUS**
Yes, it will happen.

**SANNIO**
You scum! And they say that here all men
have equality before the law.

**AESCHINUS**
Now if you've raged enough, you slave dealer,
please listen to me.

**SANNIO**
Who's the one who's raging, you or me?

**AESCHINUS**
Forget that and let's get down to business.

**SANNIO**
What business? What am I supposed to get down to?

**AESCHINUS**
Are you ready to hear your interest in this?

**SANNIO**
Absolutely, as long it's fair.

**AESCHINUS**
Right, a man who buys and sells young women wants a fair deal.

**SANNIO**
I'm a slave dealer, I admit it. I specialize in young women.
I'm the common plague of all young men, a liar, a disease.

All the same, I'm not the origin of this illegality.
Not at all.

**AESCHINUS**

My god, so you haven't exhausted your supply of illegality?

**SANNIO**

Go back to where you started, Aeschinus.                              190

**AESCHINUS**

Alright, damn you, you bought that girl for 20 minas.
You'll be paid back that much.

**SANNIO**

What? And if I refuse to sell her to you, you'll force me?

**AESCHINUS**

Not at all.

**SANNIO**

Oh, I was afraid you would.

**AESCHINUS**

And I don't think she ought to be sold.
She's a free woman. Yes, I will enter a formal plea
on her behalf to prove her free-born status.
Consider then which of two options you prefer:
take the money or start preparing to litigate.
Think it over till I get back to you, slave dealer.

*(Aeschinus goes into Micio's house.)*

**SANNIO**

Good Juppiter in the sky! It's no wonder that
being victimized by crime can drive you insane.
He dragged me from my house, shoved me around,
abducted the girl that belongs to me as I resisted him,
beat the crap out of me — a poor little man.                          200
And in exchange for these crimes
he wants me to give her up at cost.
Well then, since he so richly deserves it,
I'll make the deal; he demands his right.
All right, I will do it, just as long as he gives me the money.
Wait a minute, though, I see what will happen:
as soon as I agree to the price, he'll produce
some witness on the spot to testify that I sold her to him.
And the money's a dream:
"Soon, soon, I'll pay you tomorrow."
I could still endure that as long as he did pay me the money,

whatever the injustice. Really, I have to face the truth:
when you go into my line of business,
you've got to accept and keep quiet about
the violence of young men. Nobody's going to pay me.
None of these considerations mean a damn thing anyway.

*(Syrus enters from Micio's house.)*

**SYRUS**
*(back inside to Aeschinus)*
Yes, yes, I'll take care of everything myself.
I'll fix it so that he agrees to everything
and on top of it say that he's been treated very well.                    210

So what's this I hear, Sannio,
about your having some sort of dispute with my master?

**SANNIO**
I never saw a fight that was more unfair
than what we had today. We're both pretty exhausted:
he from beating me up and I from getting beaten up.

**SYRUS**
It was your fault.

**SANNIO**
What was I supposed to do?

**SYRUS**
You should have gratified a young man.

**SANNIO**
How could I have gratified him better?
I let him hit me in the mouth.

**SYRUS**
Come on, you want to know what I say?
Sometimes forgetting about money at the right moment
is the best way to make a profit.
Look, you fool, you were afraid that if you made
the slightest concession in your rights
and been a little more gratifying to a young man,
that you wouldn't be paid back with interest.

**SANNIO**
I do not pay cash for hope.

**SYRUS**
You'll never make any money that way.                                     220
All right, good-bye Sannio,
you just don't know how to bait a trap.

**SANNIO**
Look, I'm sure your way is better.
It's just that I have never been far-thinking enough
not to prefer whatever I could get right at the moment.

**SYRUS**
Come on, I know what you're like.
As if 20 minas mattered to you
when you could just as easily oblige him.
Besides, I've heard you're about to sail for Cyprus.

**SANNIO**
Damn.

**SYRUS**
You have a whole line of merchandise to sell there.
You've chartered a boat. I know this must weigh on your mind.
When you come back, we can talk about it further.

**SANNIO**
I will not budge.
*(to himself)*
Damn it, I'm lost. That was their hope all along
when they started this.

*(Delivery changes to unaccompanied speech.)*

**SYRUS**
*(to himself)*
He's scared. I put a stone in his shoe.

**SANNIO**
*(to himself)*
Bastards. Look at that, he's hit me
right where I'm vulnerable. I bought a whole shipment
of slave women and other goods to export to Cyprus.     230
And if I don't get there in time for the slave market,
I'll lose the whole investment. But if I let this business go
and take it up again when I return, I lose.
The negotiation will be frozen.
"You're coming now, after all this time?
Why did you allow so much time to pass?
Where have you been for so long?"
That's their strategy: it's better for me
just to give her up than to stay here long enough
to get her back or take it up when I return.

**SYRUS**

So have you figured out when you think you'll be back?

**SANNIO**

This is a tactic worthy of your household, is it?
So that's what Aeschinus is trying to do:
rob me of my girl by violence and illegality?

**SYRUS**

(aside) He's wavering.
I have just one thing to say, Sannio, see if you agree.
Rather than gambling on getting all or nothing,                    240
take half. He can scrape together 10 minas somewhere or other.

**SANNIO**

Oh, so a poor man is now in doubt about his principal?
Has he no shame? He's broken all my teeth,
and my whole head is a swollen tumor
because he beat the crap out of me.
On top of that, he's going to cheat me?
Here I draw the line.

**SYRUS**

Whatever you say. I'm sure
there's nothing further I can do before I go.

**SANNIO**

No, no, Heracles, let me ask you this, Syrus.
Whatever's happened, rather than my going to court,
just let me be repaid what I paid for her.
At cost, Syrus. And I know
that up to now you haven't enjoyed my friendship,            250
but in future you'll have reason to say
that I don't forget a favor.

**SYRUS**

I'll do my best.

(Ctesipho enters from the town.)

**SYRUS**

Well, here's Ctesipho.
He's thrilled about his girlfriend.

**SANNIO**

What about my offer?

**SYRUS**

Be patient.

(Sannio hides himself and lurks. Delivery changes to unaccompanied speech.)

**CTESIPHO**

There's great joy from someone doing you a favor.
But when the favor comes from the right man...
O my brother, my brother, what can I say in your praise?
I'm sure of this: whatever I say
is not magnificent enough to express how wonderful you are.
I judge that I have one great advantage over everybody else.
There isn't a man whose brother is
such a master of every good quality.

**SYRUS**

Ctesipho!                                                                    260

**CTESIPHO**

Syrus, where's Aeschinus?

**SYRUS**

Here at home. He's waiting for you.

**CTESIPHO**

Oh!

**SYRUS**

What is it?

**CTESIPHO**

What is it? Syrus, it's because of him that I'm now alive.
What a sweet guy! He put all of my interests ahead of his.
The fights, the gossip, my trouble, my misdeed,
he took upon himself. Nothing can top this.

The door's opening!

**SYRUS**

Wait, wait, it's your brother coming out.

*(Aeschinus enters from Micio's house.)*

**AESCHINUS**

What about that piece of filth now?

**SANNIO**

*(aside)* He means me. He doesn't have anything, does he?
Damn, I can't make it out.

**AESCHINUS**

O, glad to see you. I was looking for you.
What's happening, Ctesipho? It's all taken care of.
No more misery for you.

**CTESIPHO**

Yes, Heracles, no more misery with a brother like you.
O my Aeschinus, o my true brother.
Oh, if I praise you any more to your face
you'll think it's flattery, not gratitude.                    270

**AESCHINUS**

Go on, you silly boy, as if you and I
didn't know each other by now, Ctesipho.
I only regret finding out so late
that it was almost beyond the power
of the whole world to help you.

**CTESIPHO**

I was ashamed.

**AESCHINUS**

That's stupidity, not shame.
A little thing like that and you're ready to leave the country?
Terrible. May the gods forbid such a thing.

**CTESIPHO**

I made a mistake.

**AESCHINUS**

Well, what does our Sannio have to say?

**SYRUS**

He's calmed down.

**AESCHINUS**

I'm going to the forum to borrow the money to pay him off.
You can go in to her now, Ctesipho.

*(Ctesipho goes in Micio's house.)*
*(Sannio emerges.)*

**SANNIO**

Syrus, go ahead.

**SYRUS**

Yes, let's get going, he'll soon be on his way to Cyprus.

**SANNIO**

Not as soon as you think.
I have plenty of time right now.

**SYRUS**

You'll be paid, don't worry.

**SANNIO**

But will he pay it all back?                    280

**SYRUS**
He'll pay it all. Just shut up and follow along.

**SANNIO**
All right.

**CTESIPHO**

*(from the door)*
Hey, hey, Syrus.

**SYRUS**
What?

**CTESIPHO**
I beg you, by Heracles, pay off
that foul man as soon as possible,
so that if he gets even madder
it won't get back to my father somehow
and I'm ruined for good.

**SYRUS**
It won't happen. Courage! Go on inside
and enjoy yourself with your girlfriend while we're gone,
get the couches and everything else ready for dinner.
As soon as the business is settled,
I'll be back home with the groceries.

**CTESIPHO**
Do so. Everything's come out so well,
let's celebrate for the rest of the day.

*(Syrus and Sannio exit towards the town.)*
*(Sostrata and Canthara enter from Sostrata's house.)*

**SOSTRATA**
How is she doing now?

**CANTHARA**
How is she doing? Quite well, I think.

*(We hear Pamphila in labor.)*
O my poor dear, your labor's just starting.
*(to Sostrata)* And you're as afraid
as if you'd never been present at a childbirth,                                    290
as if you'd never had a child yourself.

**SOSTRATA**
We're in terrible trouble, we have no friends,
we're alone. And Geta's not here,
and I have no one to send for the midwife
or to bring Aeschinus here.

**CANTHARA**

Oh, he'll soon be here. He always comes,
he's never missed a day.

**SOSTRATA**

He's been my only support through these troubles.

**CANTHARA**

Consider the circumstances, mistress.
Things could not have turned out better.
She may have been raped, but he is a fine man,
of such character and heart, born of such a fine family.

**SOSTRATA**

Well, by Pollux, I suppose.
Let's just hope the gods keep him that way.

*(Geta enters from the town.)*

**GETA**

Well, it's down to this: there's nothing
that all the intelligence in all the world
can do to figure a way out of our problem.                    300
There's no help for me, for my mistress,
for my mistress's daughter. O gods!
Suddenly we're walled in by so many things that there's no way out:
rape, poverty, crime, helplessness, disgrace. What times we're living
   in!
Injustice! Sacrilege! A shameless man...!

**SOSTRATA**

O god, what's Geta so upset about?

**GETA**

....whom neither honor, nor oath, nor pity held back or restrained,
not even when the girl he shamefully and violently had his way with
is on the verge of having his baby...

**SOSTRATA**

I can't understand what he's talking about.

**CANTHARA**

Well let's find out, Sostrata.

**GETA**

...O, I'm out of my mind I'm so burning with anger.              310
There's nothing I'd like better
than having a crack at that whole family
so I could spill all my anger on them
while the wound is fresh.

I wouldn't mind a whipping
as long as I could get my vengeance on them.
First I'd strangle the old man himself
who brought up that criminal son.
And then that instigator Syrus, O, I'd tear him to shreds.
I'd get him up by the waist and smash him back to the ground
on his head to spill out his brains on the road.
I'd pluck out the eyes of the young man
and then throw him over a cliff.
The others I'll rush and drive and knock
and thrash and trample under my feet.

But I'd better stop and inform my mistress immediately.                    320

**SOSTRATA**
Let's bring him back! Geta!

**GETA**
Let me go, whoever you are.

**SOSTRATA**
It's me, Sostrata.

**GETA**
Where is she?

You're the one I'm looking for.
I need to talk to you. Perfect timing, mistress.

**SOSTRATA**
What's the matter? Why are you shaking?

**GETA**
O no...

**CANTHARA**
What are you running around for? Catch your breath, Geta.

**GETA**
We're absolutely...

**SOSTRATA**
Absolutely what?

**GETA**
Absolutely ruined. It's all over.

**SOSTRATA**
Tell me please.

**GETA**
Now...

**SOSTRATA**
What now?

**GETA**
Aeschinus...

**SOSTRATA**
What about Aeschinus?

**GETA**
He's separated himself from our family.

**SOSTRATA**
What? I can't believe it. Why?

**GETA**
He's in love with another girl.

**SOSTRATA**
God help us!

**GETA**
He makes no secret of it. He carried her off
himself from the sex-slave dealer, all in the open.

**SOSTRATA**
Are you sure?

**GETA**
I'm sure. I saw it with my my own eyes, Sostrata.

**SOSTRATA**
O, I'm ruined. What can you depend on anymore?                    330
Whom can you trust? Our Aeschinus, the life of us all,
in whom we placed our hopes and dreams?
who swore that he couldn't live a single day without her?
who said he'd put his baby in his father's lap,
and thereby implore his father to let him marry her?

**GETA**
Mistress, stop crying and start thinking about what to do!
Are we just going to let this go by
or are we going to tell someone about it?

**CANTHARA**
Man, man, are you in your right mind?
You think this ought to be spread around?

**GETA**
I for one don't think so.
In the first place, the facts show
that he is now estranged from us.

If we bring it out in the open now,
he'll deny it, that I know,
and your reputation and your daughter's life will be at risk.          340
Secondly, even if he admits the whole thing,
it's not in the girl's interest to be married
to a man who's in love with someone else.
Whatever you say, no, we need to keep quiet.

**SOSTRATA**
Not for the whole world, I won't.

**GETA**
What will you do?

**SOSTRATA**
I'll tell.

**CANTHARA**
O, Sostrata, do you see what you're doing?

**SOSTRATA**
Things can't get worse than they are now.
First, she has no dowry. And then besides that
what was hers in place of a dowry has been lost.
She cannot be married as a virgin. There's one way: on my side as
    witness
is the ring he let her have. Since I know well
that I bear no responsibility for my daughter's fault
and that no money has been paid
or any business transacted unworthy of me or my daughter,
Geta, I will go to court.

**GETA**
All right then, your way is better, I admit it.          350

**SOSTRATA**
You go immediately to our kinsman Hegio.
He can stand for her in court.
Tell him the whole story from beginning to end.
When my dear husband Simulus was alive,
Hegio was his best friend.
He's always taken care of us.

**GETA**
Well, yes, by Heracles, he's the one to turn to.

**SOSTRATA**
And you, hurry up, Canthara dear, run,
summon the midwife so she's here the moment she's needed.

*(Geta and Canthara exit towards town. Sostrata goes into her house.)*
*(Enter Demea from town. Delivery changes to unaccompanied speech.)*

**DEMEA**

Damn! I have been informed that my son Ctesipho
had a part with Aeschinus in carrying off that girl.
That's the one disaster left to me to suffer,
that it's possible for the son that's still worth something
to be led by the other into debauchery.
Where am I to look for him?
Drawn to some prostitutes' tavern, I presume.
The profligate tempted him there, that I know.                   360

*(Syrus with other slaves enters from town with the groceries.)*
Well, it's Syrus. Now I will find out immediately
where he is. But, Heracles, he's part of that flock.
If he senses I'm looking for him, that coffin meat
will never tell. I won't reveal what I'm after.

**SYRUS**

*(sees Demea but doesn't let on; to the other slaves)*
I've just told my master the whole story.
I never saw anyone happier.

**DEMEA**

Juppiter almighty, what an idiot!

**SYRUS**

He praised his son, and thanked me
for having given him that advice.

**DEMEA**

I'm going to burst.

**SYRUS**

He counted out the money then and there.
In addition he gave me half a mina for a little dinner party.       370
That I've spent quite nicely according to his wishes.

**DEMEA**

Quite! If you want some dirty business
taken care of properly, ask him.

**SYRUS**

Well, Demea, I didn't see you there. What's going on?

**DEMEA**

What's going on? I'll never cease being amazed
at how you people live.

**SYRUS**

Absolutely, it's incompetent. To be honest, it's absurd.

*(inside to slaves)*
Clean these fish carefully, Dromo.
Except for that nice big conger.
Let him play in the water for a little while.
We won't fillet it till we're ready. Not before.

**DEMEA**

This is a scandal.

**SYRUS**

I'm not pleased either; I often protest.
Stephanio, make sure those salted fish are nicely soaked.            380

**DEMEA**

Gods in heaven, is he doing it on purpose,
or does he think it will be to his credit if he corrupts his son?
O me, I can see the day when he will have to run away
in poverty and become a mercenary abroad.

**SYRUS**

Ah, Demea, that is wisdom.
To forsee not only what is before your feet
but to forsee what is to come.

**DEMEA**

So, is that instrumentalist still in your home?

**SYRUS**

Yes, she is.

**DEMEA**

He's going to keep her there, is that it?

**SYRUS**

I think so. Our household is crazy enough.

**DEMEA**

That these things go on!                                            390

**SYRUS**

The father is lenient and permissive.
It's foolish and wicked.

**DEMEA**

My brother shames me and angers me.

**SYRUS**

That's the difference between you two, Demea,
the enormous difference. And I'm not saying that

just because you're standing here in front of me.
You, every bit of you, is wisdom itself;
he's an insubstantial nothing.
You wouldn't have allowed your son to behave that way.

**DEMEA**

Wouldn't have allowed it?
Wouldn't I have smelled it out six whole months
before he started anything?

**SYRUS**

No need to tell me how vigilant you are.

**DEMEA**

If only he remain as he is now.

**SYRUS**

As each of you two wishes his son, so it is.

**DEMEA**

What about my son? Have you seen him today?                    400

**SYRUS**

Your son? *(to himself)* I'll herd him off to the country.
*(to Demea)* I think for a while now
he's been doing something on the farm.

**DEMEA**

You're sure he's there?

**SYRUS**

I walked out there with him myself.

**DEMEA**

Excellent. I was afraid he was hanging around here.

**SYRUS**

He was quite angry.

**DEMEA**

What about?

**SYRUS**

He was taking his brother to task about the girl
right out in the forum.

**DEMEA**

Is that so?

**SYRUS**

Oh, he didn't mince words.
Just when the money was changing hands,
your son appeared unexpectedly and began to protest:

"Aeschinus, you, disgracing yourself!
you, bringing shame upon our family!"

**DEMEA**

Oh, I weep for joy!

**SYRUS**

"You're not wasting this money, you're wasting your very life."     410

**DEMEA**

Bless him. He's a chip off the old block.

**SYRUS**

(to himself) Whoa!

**DEMEA**

Syrus, that son of mine is just full of those moral precepts.

**SYRUS**

No wonder. He had someone at home to learn them from.

**DEMEA**

One does one's best. Careful of every detail.
Constant training. Altogether I tell him
to examine the ways of life of everyone as if in a mirror
and to draw from others an example for himself. "Do this."

**SYRUS**

Quite right.

**DEMEA**

"Don't do that."

**SYRUS**

Well done.

**DEMEA**

"This does you credit."

**SYRUS**

Exactly.

**DEMEA**

"This does you shame."

**SYRUS**

Very fine.

**DEMEA**

And furthermore...

**SYRUS**

Gods, I don't have time right now to listen to this.     420
I found some really good buys at the fish market
and I have to make sure they're not ruined in the preparation.

You know, it's just as much a disgrace for us
not to take care of our things as for you masters
not to take care of the things you just mentioned.
As far as I can, I give moral precepts to my fellow slaves
in the same manner: "Too much salt." "Too well done."
"Not properly cleaned." "That's right. Remember to do it that way
    again."
I do the best I can, given my wisdom.
Altogether, Demea, I tell them to examine
the dishes as if a mirror and I teach them what they must do.
I realize these things that we do are silly.           430
As a man is, so must you treat him. Will that be all?

**DEMEA**

Get yourself a better mind.

**SYRUS**

You'll be going to the country?

**DEMEA**

Right away.

**SYRUS**

Yes, why spend time in the city
where you can give good moral instruction and nobody obeys it.

*(Syrus exits into house.)*

**DEMEA**

Well, of course, I'm off to the country
when my son whom I came to find has gone there already.
He's the only thing I care about. I'm concerned for him.
Just as my brother wishes it. Let him look after the other the way he
    wants.

*(Hegio and Geta enter.)*

Well, who is this I see? It's Hegio, a man from my hometown.
If my eyes don't deceive me it certainly is. Ah, my friend from child-
    hood.          440
Good gods, there aren't many citizens of his kind left.
Old-fashioned virtue and honor.
Public affairs are in good hands with him.
I'm happy when I see what's left of his kind still here.
There's still some joy in life.
I'll go up to say hello and talk with him.

**HEGIO**

Good gods, it's a shameful crime, Geta.
What are you telling me?

**GETA**
It happened.

**HEGIO**
It's hard to believe a crime so unbecoming refinement
could have sprung from that family.
Aeschinus, you have not taken after your father.                    450

**DEMEA**
Obviously he's heard about the music girl.
Even though he's not family
it pains him that the father cares nothing.
O, I wish he were here listening to this!

**HEGIO**
If they don't do the right thing,
they won't get away with it.

**GETA**
We place all our hopes in you, Hegio.
We have only you. You are her champion,
you are her father. As he lay dying
my old master entrusted us to you.
If you desert us, we are lost.

**HEGIO**
Don't even think it. I will not let you down.
I shoulder my responsibilities.

**DEMEA**
I will go up to him. My fondest greetings, Hegio.          460

**HEGIO**
Ah, hello, Demea, just the one I was looking for.

**DEMEA**
Why is that?

**HEGIO**
Your elder son Aeschinus,
whom you gave to your brother to adopt,
has not discharged his duty
as an honest man and as a man of refinement.

**DEMEA**
And how is that?

**HEGIO**
You knew our friend and contemporary Simulus?

**DEMEA**
Of course.

**HEGIO**

Your son has raped his virgin daughter.

**DEMEA**

I see.

**HEGIO**

Wait, Demea, you have not yet heard the most serious charge.

**DEMEA**

Can there be anything worse?

**HEGIO**

Yes, there is. Part of it can be forgiven.
He was overwhelmed: night, desire, wine, he's a young man.      470
It's human nature. When he realized what he had done,
on his own he went to the mother of girl,
in tears, begging, pleading, promising,
swearing that he would marry her.
He was forgiven, the matter was not publicized,
they took his word.
The girl became pregnant from this violation.
She's at the end of her ninth month.
That honest gentleman of ours, please the gods,
has now purchased a music-girl to live with.
He's abandoned the other one.

**DEMEA**

Are you quite sure?

**HEGIO**

The mother of the girl can testify.
There's the girl. There's the fact that she's pregnant.
And besides that there's Geta here,
who, as slaves go, is rather reliable and energetic.      480
He alone supports and sustains the family.
Take him off, have him tortured and interrogated.

**GETA**

Yes, by Heracles, torture me if it's not the truth, Demea.
And Aeschinus won't deny it. Ask him yourself.

**DEMEA**

I feel ashamed. I don't know what to do or how to respond.

**PAMPHILA**

(*voice from the house*)
Oh, Oh, the pain, the pain is killing me.

Juno Lucina, help me!
Save me I beg you!

**HEGIO**

Well, she's not about to give birth?

**GETA**

Yes, she is, Hegio.

**HEGIO**

Listen to me, Demea, she's appealing
to the honor of your family.
Please do willingly what honor compels you to do.    490
I pray the gods that what you do
will bring credit to all of you.
But if your intentions are different, Demea,
with the utmost energy I will defend that girl
and the memory of my departed friend.
He was my kinsman, we were brought up together
from our youngest boyhood. We were together
serving in the army and at home.
We endured together harsh poverty.
Whatever struggle be required now, I will endure it.
I will work hard, I will go to court,
I will even lay down my life before I desert that family.
What do you have to say?

**DEMEA**

Hegio, I will speak with my brother.

**HEGIO**

Alright, Demea, but have this in mind:    500
the easier your life is, the more powerful you are,
the wealthier, the more well off,
the higher the status you enjoy,
the more you are obligated by what is just and right
to recognize and act upon what is just and right,
if you want a reputation for respectability.

**DEMEA**

Return to us. All that is just and right will be done.

**HEGIO**

That would be a credit to you. Geta, take me inside to Sostrata.

*(Hegio and Geta go in Sostrata's house.)*

**DEMEA**

This is exactly what I predicted.

I only wish this were the end of it.
This excessive permissiveness will surely
end up in some terrible catastrophe.
I'm going to be sick. I'll go find my brother
and vomit this story right out to him.                                    510

*(Demea exits towards the town.)*
*(Hegio enters from Sostrata's house.)*

**HEGIO**
Don't worry, Sostrata. Do what you can to comfort her.
I will talk to Micio if he's in the forum
and tell him from beginning to end all that's happened.
If it happens that he intends to do his duty,
let him do it.
If he has some other thought in mind on this matter,
let him give me an answer.
I will know what I have to do.

*(Hegio exits towards the town.)*
*(Syrus and Ctesipho enter from Micio's house. Delivery changes to
accompanied speech.)*

**CTESIPHO**
So my father has gone to the country?

**SYRUS**
A while ago.

**CTESIPHO**
Please tell me he's gone home.

**SYRUS**
He's at your farm. At this very moment
I'm sure he's occupied with some piece of work.

**CTESIPHO**
I hope he is. As long as he doesn't hurt himself,
I hope he gets so exhausted that he can't
get out of bed for the next three days.                                    520

**SYRUS**
I hope so too, or for something even better.

**CTESIPHO**
Yes, all I want to do is spend
the whole day as I began it, in pleasure.
And what I really hate about that country place
is that it's so near. If it were farther away,
night could overtake him before he had a chance to return here.

As it is, when he doesn't find me he'll run right back here,
I'm sure of that. He'll ask me where I've been:
"I haven't seen you all day." What'll I say?

**SYRUS**
Nothing comes to mind?

**CTESIPHO**
Nothing at all.

**SYRUS**
The more fool you are.
Don't you have a client, a friend, a guest friend?

**CTESIPHO**
Yes, so...

**SYRUS**
Can't say you had business with them?                    530

**CTESIPHO**
When I didn't? I can't say that.

**SYRUS**
Yes you can.

**CTESIPHO**
During the day, but what if I spend the night here,
what reason can I give, Syrus?

**SYRUS**
Ah, yes, I've often wished you could get by with
claiming to conduct business with friends at night.
Just relax; I've got the man all figured out.
When he's at his hottest, I can make him as gentle as a sheep.

**CTESIPHO**
How do you do that?

**SYRUS**
He loves to hear you being praised.
In front of him, I make you out to be a god.
I tell the virtues.

**CTESIPHO**
Mine?

**SYRUS**
Yours. Right away, the old man cries like a baby for joy.

*(Syrus sees Demea approaching the house.)*

**SYRUS**
Well, there you go.

**CTESIPHO**
What?

**SYRUS**
The wolf in the story.

**CTESIPHO**
It's my father?

**SYRUS**
It's your father.

**CTESIPHO**
Syrus, what are we going to do?

**SYRUS**
Go hide somewhere, I'll take care of it.

**CTESIPHO**
If he asks, you never saw me. You hear?

**SYRUS**
Can you shut up?

*(Demea enters from the town.)*

**DEMEA**
I swear, I'm a wretched man.                                540
I can't find my brother anywhere on earth.
Besides that, while I was looking for him,
I saw one of my hired hands from the farm.
He told me my son isn't out on the farm.
I don't know what to do.

**CTESIPHO**
Syrus.

**SYRUS**
What is it?

**CTESIPHO**
Is he looking for me?

**SYRUS**
Yes.

**CTESIPHO**
Oh no.

**SYRUS**
Just be brave.

**DEMEA**
What the hell does this bad luck mean?
I can't figure it out, except I believe

that the reason I was born is to endure pain and misery.
I'm the first to hear about our problems,
I'm the first to get wise to everything,
I'm the first to announce the bad news.
When something happens, I'm the only one who troubles himself.

**SYRUS**
Don't make me laugh. He says he's the first to know;
he's the only one who doesn't know.

**DEMEA**
Now I return; perhaps my brother is home.

**CTESIPHO**
Syrus, look, don't let him just rush right inside here.                    550

**SYRUS**
Can't you be quiet? I'll take care of it.

**CTESIPHO**
Heracles, I will not trust you with that.
I will lock myself up with her in one of the slave rooms.
That's safest.

*(Ctesipho goes in the house.)*

**SYRUS**
Alright, I'll get him out of here anyway.

**DEMEA**
Well, the scoundrel Syrus.

**SYRUS**
I swear to the gods there's nobody who can endure it
if things go on like this.
I would simply like to know how many masters I have.
What a pain this is!

**DEMEA**
What's he yapping about? What does he want?
Tell me, my good man, is my brother home?

**SYRUS**
Why the hell are you calling me "my good man"? I'm finished.

**DEMEA**
What's with you?

**SYRUS**
You're asking what's with me?
Ctesipho beat me up with his fists
almost to death. And the music girl.

**DEMEA**
What are you telling me?

**SYRUS**
See, look how he cut my lip.

**DEMEA**
Why?                                                                    560

**SYRUS**
He said that I was the instigator of buying the girl.

**DEMEA**
Didn't you tell me that he had left here for the country?

**SYRUS**
I did; but he came back here, crazed.
He showed no mercy. Not to feel shame
at beating up an old man!
The boy I used to cradle in my arms
when he was just a little boy.

**DEMEA**
Well done, Ctesipho! You take after your father.
Yes, I judge you a man!

**SYRUS**
Well done? If he's smart, he'll keep his fists
to himself after this.

**DEMEA**
Bravely done!

**SYRUS**
Very brave, when he takes advantage of a poor woman
and me, a poor little slave who didn't dare hit back.
Very brave, indeed!

**DEMEA**
It couldn't have been better.
He understands what I do—
that you are the root of this problem.
Is my brother home?

**SYRUS**
He's not.

**DEMEA**
I wonder where I might find him.

**SYRUS**
I know where he is, but I will never tell you.                          570

**DEMEA**
What did you just say to me?

**SYRUS**
What I just said to you.

**DEMEA**
I'm going to bash your head in.

*(He threatens violence.)*

**SYRUS**
Well, I don't know the man's name, but I know the place.

**DEMEA**
Tell me then.

**SYRUS**
Do you know the portico down by the meat market?

**DEMEA**
Of course.

**SYRUS**
Go straight up that street. When you get there,
the Hill is right down in front of you. Down you go.
Then on this side, there's a shrine.
Right next to it is an alley-way.

**DEMEA**
Which one?

**SYRUS**
Where there's that big wild-fig tree.

**DEMEA**
I know it.

**SYRUS**
Go that way.

**DEMEA**
Wait a minute, that alley's a dead end.

**SYRUS**
Yes, yes, you're right. Ah, you must think I'm an idiot.
I made a mistake. Go back to the portico.
There's a much faster way and less of a chance            580
of missing the street. You know the house
of that rich man Cratinus?

**DEMEA**
I do.

**SYRUS**

When you go past it, go left and straight along the street.
When you get to the sanctuary of Diana, turn right.
Before you come to the city gate, just at the watering troughs,
there's a bakery and opposite that there's a workshop.
He's there.

**DEMEA**

What's he doing there?

**SYRUS**

He's ordering some outdoor couches to be made with holmoak° legs.

**DEMEA**

For one of your drinking parties, well that's just fine.
I will go find him immediately.

**SYRUS**

Go. Please.

*(Demea exits towards the town.)*

**SYRUS**

I'll give you today the exercise that you deserve,
you old funeral feast!
Aeschinus is annoyingly late.
Our dinner is spoiling. Ctesipho is totally in love.
Now I'll look out for myself. I will now go off                    590
and sample every little tasty morsel
and ladling out one bowl of wine after another
I'll stretch out this day.

*(Syrus exits into Micio's house.)*

*(Enter Micio and Hegio from the town.)*

**MICIO**

I see no reason for you
to think especially well of me in this matter, Hegio.
I am doing my duty. I am correcting the wrong we caused.
Surely you didn't think me one of those people
who think that they are being wronged
if you accuse them of the wrong that they have done,
and on top of that accuse you.
You're not thanking me for not behaving that way?

**HEGIO**

Not at all. It never entered my mind
that you were other than you are. But please,

---

° holmoak = ilex (holly)

would you come with me to see the girl's mother,
and tell her exactly what you told me;
what made her suspicious Aeschinus did for his brother,          600
the music girl is his.

**MICIO**

If that's the right thing to do,
or you think it's necessary, let's go.

**HEGIO**

Good. You'll relieve her. She's been wracked
with pain and anxiety over this.
And you will have performed your duty.
But if you don't think so,
I will tell her myself what you told me.

**MICIO**

No, no, on the contrary, I will go.

**HEGIO**

Good. Those who aren't quite so well off
are just a little bit—I don't know—more suspicious.
They are ready to take offence at an imagined insult.
They think they're trapped because of their lack of resources.
To explain yourself in person is therefore the more satisfying course.

**MICIO**

Yes, you're quite right.

**HEGIO**

Let's go.

**MICIO**

By all means.

*(Micio and Hegio go into Sostrata's house.)*

*(Aeschinus enters from the town. Accompaniment continues. Polymetric song.)*

**AESCHINUS**

I'm in torture.                                                 610
Suddenly faced with such a disaster.
I don't know what to do, how to act.
My limbs are weak with fear.
My heart is stunned with terror.
My mind is empty of advice.
Ah, how to get clear of the madness?
I'm under suspicion, a natural one.
Sostrata thinks I bought the music-girl for myself.

That crone made the accusation against me.

*(Polymetric song ends. Accompaniment continues.)*

She had been sent to bring the midwife,
and I ran into her. I was asking how Pamphila was doing,
if she was about to give birth, if she needed the midwife.
She screams at me: "Away from me, away,                             620
we want nothing more to do with you, Aeschinus.
You've deceived us long enough.
We've had enough of your broken promises."
I said, "What in the world are you talking about?"
She says, "Good-bye and good riddance.
Have whatever girl you want!"
I immediately understood what they thought I had done,
but I had to hold back. If I had said anything about my brother
to that old gossip it would have been all over town.
What should I do now? Say the girl belongs to my brother?
That cannot be made public.
But that aside — it's still possible that it won't get out —
they'd never believe what actually happened.
There are so many things that look like the truth
mixed in with the truth. I was the one who carried her off;
I was the one who paid off the slave dealer for her;
she was taken into my house.
I admit that what is happening is all my fault.
As bad as the situation was,
I should have told my father about it.
I should have gotten his permission to marry her.                   630
I've been slow up to now. Wake up, Aeschinus.
First priority: go to them, clear myself.

I'll go up to the door. I can't.
I always feel so tense when I knock at this door.
Hello. Hello. It's Aeschinus. Open the door, somebody.

Someone's coming out. I 'll hide over here.

*(Micio enters from Sostrata's house. Sostrata at the door.)*

**MICIO**

All of you do as I have told you, Sostrata.
I will see Aeschinus to let him know
what has been decided.

Where's the person who was knocking at the door?

**AESCHINUS**

Gods, it's my father. I'm lost.

**MICIO**

Aeschinus!

*(Delivery changes to unaccompanied speech.)*

**AESCHINUS**

*(to himself)* What's he doing here?

**MICIO**

Was it you who just knocked on this door?
*(to himself)* No answer.
Why shouldn't I have a little fun with him?
He deserves it since he didn't tell me about any of this.          640
*(to Aeschinus)* You have nothing to say to me?

**AESCHINUS**

Not about knocking on the door, as far as my knowledge goes.

**MICIO**

Well. I was wondering what business you could have here.
*(to himself)* He's blushing. It will be all right.

**AESCHINUS**

Well please tell me, father, what brought you there.

**MICIO**

Nothing to do with me. A friend of mine
brought me from the forum to conduct a negotiation for him.

**AESCHINUS**

What is that?

**MICIO**

I will tell you. Some women live next door
who aren't so well off. I don't believe you know them.
I'm sure you don't. They moved here not too long ago.

**AESCHINUS**

And...

**MICIO**

There's an unmarried girl and her mother.          650

**AESCHINUS**

Go on.

**MICIO**

This girl has been orphaned of her father.
My friend is next of kin, and as you know,
the law requires him to marry her off to someone.

**AESCHINUS**
Damn.

**MICIO**
What is it?

**AESCHINUS**
Nothing, fine, go on.

**MICIO**
He's come to take her with him. He lives in Miletus.

**AESCHINUS**
I see. He's come to take the girl with him.

**MICIO**
That is so.

**AESCHINUS**
Across the sea to Miletus?

**MICIO**
Yes.

**AESCHINUS**
I feel sick. And the women, what do they say?

**MICIO**
What do you think? Of course some nonsense.
The mother told a story about a child and some other man.
She didn't give his name.
He was first, she said, and her daughter
shouldn't be given to the man from Miletus.

**AESCHINUS**
What, you don't think these claims are just, do you?                    660

**MICIO**
No.

**AESCHINUS**
Really, you don't? Then will he take her away, father?

**MICIO**
Why shouldn't he?

**AESCHINUS**
The matter has been handled by all of you
in a way that's uncivilized and pitiless,
and, not only that, if I must speak more frankly,
in a way that's lacking in generosity of spirit.

**MICIO**
In what way?

**AESCHINUS**

You're asking me? How in the world do you think
that poor lovesick man is going to feel —
the first man who was intimate with her,
and for all I know still loves her desperately —
when he sees her snatched away from him
right in front of his eyes?
A terrible crime, father.

**MICIO**

How do you figure? Who betrothed her?                           670
Who gave her in marriage? Who married her?
Who gave consent and had legal authority to do so?
Why did the man marry another man's wife?

**AESCHINUS**

And is an unmarried girl of that age
supposed to sit at home waiting for a kinsman
to arrive from Miletus?
That's what justice demanded you to say, father,
and the position you ought to have defended.

**MICIO**

Ridiculous. Was I supposed to argue the case
against the man on whose behalf I had come to court?
Anyway, what business is this of ours, Aeschinus?
What do we have to do with them? Let's go home.

*(Delivery changes to accompanied speech.)*

What's wrong? Why are you crying?

**AESCHINUS**

Father, please, listen.

**MICIO**

Aeschinus, I heard all about it.                               680
I know. I love you.
All the more I care about what you do.

**AESCHINUS**

May I always deserve your love,
as long as you live, my father,
as surely as to ackowledge what I have done
pains me deeply and shames me.

**MICIO**

Heracles, I believe it.
I know that you are a man born with a generous and free spirit.

But I'm afraid you are excessively careless.
Tell me what city you think you're living in.
You have violated a virgin whom it was not lawful for you to touch.
Right away that's a serious transgression.
But it's human. It's often happened before,
even with honest men. But after it happened,
tell me, you couldn't have considered
or planned very carefully what you should have done,       690
how you should have done it.
If you were ashamed to tell me yourself,
did you think about how I would find out?
While you were hesitating, nine months went by.
You have betrayed yourself and that poor young woman
and your child, as far as it was in your capacity.
What, did you think that the gods
would do your work for you while you slept?
That without your making arrangements
she would be magically conducted in marriage home to your bed-
    room?
I would not wish to see you as lazy in other affairs
as you have been in this. Don't worry, you'll marry her.

**AESCHINUS**
What?

**MICIO**
I say don't worry.

**AESCHINUS**
Father, please, you're not joking.

**MICIO**
Why should I be?

**AESCHINUS**
I don't know. It's just that I want this
to be true so badly, I'm all the more afraid.

**MICIO**
Go. Pray the gods' favor in bringing home your wife. Go.

**AESCHINUS**
What? My wife? Now?       700

**MICIO**
Now.

**AESCHINUS**
Now?

**MICIO**
Now. As soon as you can.

**AESCHINUS**
May the gods curse me if I don't love you more than my own eyes.

**MICIO**
What? More than her?

**AESCHINUS**
Well, just as much.

**MICIO**
That's kind of you.

**AESCHINUS**
Wait a minute. Where's that Milesian?

**MICIO**
He's dead. He's gone. He sailed away on a ship.
What are you waiting for?

**AESCHINUS**
You go, father, you pray to the gods.
You are a much better man than I,
and I know for certain
that they're much more likely to listen to you.

**MICIO**
Well, we'll make the necessary preparations.
Do what I've told you if you know what's good for you.

*(Micio goes in his house.)*

**AESCHINUS**
Can you imagine it?
Is this to be a father or is this to be a son?
If he were my brother or my friend,
could he have done more perfectly what I wanted him to do?
Isn't he a man to be loved, just to be hugged.

Hmm. Because of his kindness, 710
I have this great desire not to do carelessly
anything he doesn't want. I will be on guard
not to displease him. But what am I waiting for?
I don't want to be the obstacle to my own wedding.

*(Aeschinus goes into his house.)*

*(Demea enters from town.)*

*(Delivery changes to unaccompanied speech.)*

**DEMEA**
I'm exhausted from walking.
Juppiter damn you and your directions, Syrus!
I've crawled over the whole town:
the city gate, the watering troughs, everywhere.
There was no workshop there,
nobody said they had seen my brother.
Now I'm absolutely going to blockade this house until he returns.
*(Micio enters from his house.)*

**MICIO**
*(speaking inside)*
I will go over and say that we're pretty much ready.

**DEMEA**
Well here he is.
I've been looking for you a long time, Micio.                    720

**MICIO**
What for?

**DEMEA**
I bring you other monstrous crimes
committed by that young man of yours.

**MICIO**
Oh gods.

**DEMEA**
New crimes, capital offenses.

**MICIO**
Now wait a minute.

**DEMEA**
You don't know the kind of man we're dealing with.

**MICIO**
Yes I do.

**DEMEA**
Oh, you fool, you're dreaming
that I'm talking about that music girl.
The offense is against a citizen, a virgin.

**MICIO**
I know.

**DEMEA**
O ho, you know and you let this go on?

**MICIO**
Why shouldn't I?

**DEMEA**
Don't you ever just start screaming?
Don't you ever just go mad?

**MICIO**
No. I might have wished —

**DEMEA**
A child has been born.

**MICIO**
May the gods bless!

**DEMEA**
The girl has nothing.

**MICIO**
I've heard.

**DEMEA**
And she must be married without a dowry.

**MICIO**
Quite.

**DEMEA**
What's going to happen?

**MICIO**
What the situation requires.                                    730
The girl will be moved from that house to this.

**DEMEA**
O Juppiter, is that necessary?

**MICIO**
What more can I do?

**DEMEA**
What more can you do?
If the situation doesn't cause you genuine pain,
you can act human and pretend that it does.

**MICIO**
Well, I've already betrothed the girl to him.
The matter is settled. There will be a wedding.
I've removed all their cause for apprehension.
That is even more human.

**DEMEA**
But are you happy with it, Micio?

**MICIO**

No, not if I could change it. But since I can't,
I'm happy with it. Living our lives is like playing with dice:
If the throw you need doesn't fall,                          740
what is given by chance you can put right with art.

**DEMEA**

Put it right? With your art, as you call it,
you've wasted 20 minas on the music girl,
whom you now must sell to I don't know whom,
if not for a price, then for free.

**MICIO**

She doesn't have to be sold
and indeed I'm not eager to sell her.

**DEMEA**

What are you going to do then?

**MICIO**

She will remain in my house.

**DEMEA**

Holy gods! A concubine and the mother of the household
together in one house!

**MICIO**

Why not?

**DEMEA**

Do you really believe that you are in your right mind?

**MICIO**

I think so.

**DEMEA**

So help me gods, I understand.                              750
You want to sing again and again to her accompaniment!

**MICIO**

Why not?

**DEMEA**

And the new bride will learn the same songs?

**MICIO**

Quite.

**DEMEA**

And you will dance on a rope between the two?

**MICIO**

Yes.

**DEMEA**
Yes?

**MICIO**
And you will join us if the need arises.

**DEMEA**
Good gods, aren't you ashamed of yourself?

**MICIO**
Alright, alright, Demea. Enough.
Calm yourself down, and be as pleasant and festive
as the occasion demands; it's the wedding of your son.
I'm going to them, then I'll come back.

*(Micio goes into the house of Sostrata.)*

**DEMEA**
O Juppiter, what a life! What morals! What insanity!
A wife without a dowry is coming. A music girl lives here.
A house of wasteful extravagance!                              760
A young man spoiled with luxury!
A maniac old man!
Salvation herself could not save this household if she wanted to.

*(Syrus enters from Micio's house, drunk.)*

**SYRUS**
I swear, little Syrus, you've taken care of yourself nicely,
and discharged the office of slave beautifully.
OK. Now that I've stuffed myself on everything,
I think I'd like to take a walk.

**DEMEA**
Look at that! An example of the discipline of the house.

**SYRUS**
Look, here's our old man. What's going on?
What are you so upset about?

**DEMEA**
Scoundrel!

**SYRUS**
Hey, enough! So, Wisdom herself, you're pouring out your sayings.

**DEMEA**
If you belonged to me...                                       770

**SYRUS**
You'd be a rich man, Demea,
and you would have put your affairs on a strong foundation.

**DEMEA**

I ought to make an example of you to the whole household.

**SYRUS**

For what? What have I done?

**DEMEA**

You're asking me? In the very midst of trouble,
in the very midst of huge disgrace
that has hardly yet been settled,
you're drunk, you scoundrel,
as if celebrating a great achievement.

**SYRUS**

Well, I'm sorry I came outside.

**DROMO**

(calling from the door)
Hey Syrus, Ctesipho wants you.

**SYRUS**

Alright.

**DEMEA**

What did he say about Ctesipho?

**SYRUS**

Nothing.

**DEMEA**

Hey, you jail meat, is Ctesipho here?

**SYRUS**

He's not.

**DEMEA**

Why did he use his name?

**SYRUS**

It's somebody else, just some guy who's staying with us.
Do you know him?

**DEMEA**

I will soon.

**SYRUS**

What are you doing? Where are you going?                    780

**DEMEA**

Let me go.

**SYRUS**

Don't get up, I say.

**DEMEA**

    I'll whip your hide if you don't let go of me.
    Or would you prefer that I knock your brains on the pavement?

    *(Demea goes free and goes into Micio's house.)*

**SYRUS**

    Well, he's gone. Not such a welcome guest to the wedding party,
    especially to Ctesipho. What should I do now?
    Until the riot calms down,
    I think it's best to find some corner
    and sleep off this little bit of wine. That's what I'll do.

    *(Syrus goes into Micio's house.)*

    *(Micio enters from Sostrata's house.)*

**MICIO**

    *(inside)*
    As I've said, everything's ready for you now, Sostrata,
    whenever you like.

    *(Demea enters from Micio's house.)*
    Who's that slamming around my door?

**DEMEA**

    Great gods, what am I to do? How am I to act?
    What cry, what complaint can I make?
    O heaven, o earth, o Neptune's seas!          790

**MICIO**

    There you have it. He's found out,
    that's what he's screaming about. It's all over.
    Now we're in trouble. I'd better go to the rescue.

**DEMEA**

    There he is, the common pimp for both our sons.

**MICIO**

    Would you please get a hold on your anger
    and come back to your senses.

**DEMEA**

    Alright, I've got a hold, I've come back,
    I'll stop the curses. Let's look at the situation.
    Was it agreed between us — and the proposal even came from you —
    that you would not interfere with my raising my son
    nor would I interfere with your raising yours? Yes?

**MICIO**

    That was the agreement, I don't deny it.

**DEMEA**

Then why is he now drinking in your house?
Why do you put my son up in your house? 800
Why have you bought him a girlfriend, Micio?
Isn't it fair that I have my rights from you as well as you
have yours from me? I don't interfere with your son,
you don't interfere with mine.

**MICIO**

That's not quite right.

**DEMEA**

No?

**MICIO**

There's an old saying: friends hold all in common.

**DEMEA**

Clever! But now's a little late for speeches like that.

**MICIO**

Listen to me for a little, Demea, without losing your temper.
In the first place, if it's the money
the boys spend that annoys you, think of it this way.
Long ago, you were bringing up your two boys within your means,
figuring that your resources would be enough for them both. 810
I dare say you also thought that I would marry.
Now stick to that same plan: build up, work, save,
leave them as much as you can for an inheritance.
That's your heritage.
Let them use my resources as an utterly unexpected windfall.
Nothing is lost from your capital.
The money that comes from me, count as pure profit.
If you allow yourself to consider this accurately, Demea,
you'll stop being a pain to me and to yourself and to them.

**DEMEA**

I'm not talking about the money, 820
it's the way they live their lives.

**MICIO**

Wait, I know, I was coming to that.
There are many indications in a man
from which a conclusion can easily be drawn.
For example, when two people are doing the same thing
you can often say, "It's dangerous for this one to do something,
but not for the other one."
Not that the action itself is different,

but the two doing the action...
Now I see in our two boys indications
that make me confident they will turn out the way we want them to.
I see that they have sense, understanding,
inhibition at the right time, love for each other.
Allow their spirit and character to grow freely,
and you know that you can bring them back at any time.
You may be afraid that nevertheless                                    830
they will be a little too careless in financial matters.
My dear Demea, in all other matters we grow wiser with age.
This is the only flaw that growing old bestows on a man:
we all care much too much about money,
on which point age will make them sharp enough.

**DEMEA**

Just be careful, Micio, that this fine philosophy of yours
and your permissiveness don't ruin us.

**MICIO**

Quiet, it won't happen. Forget about it.
Just today, let me tell you what to do.
Wipe the scowl off your face.

**DEMEA**

Well, so the occasion requires. I must do it.                          840
But tomorrow at dawn I will return to the country with my son.

**MICIO**

In the middle of the night, I imagine. Just be pleasant today.

**DEMEA**

And that music girl I'll drag off with me as well.

**MICIO**

A good strategy. That way you'll bind him to the farm.
Just make sure *she* doesn't run away.

**DEMEA**

I'll take care of that. I'll have her cooking
and grinding corn, she'll be full of ash and smoke and meal.
And not only that, I'll have her collecting straw
under the noonday sun. I'll make her as sunburnt
and black as a piece of charcoal.

**MICIO**

Good idea. Now I see you have some sense.                              850
And if I were you, I would then force him to sleep with her.

**DEMEA**
Are you mocking me? You're lucky to have that disposition.
I take things to heart.

**MICIO**
So you're going to go on?

**DEMEA**
No, no. I'm finished. I'm finished.

**MICIO**
Go ahead into my house then,
and let us enjoy the day as it ought to be enjoyed.

*(Micio exits into his house. Delivery changes to accompanied speech.)*

**DEMEA**
No man has ever calculated up
the profits and losses of his life
so accurately that circumstances,
age, experience, don't add something new,
don't teach some new lesson.
What you thought you knew, you don't know.
What you thought most important, with experience you reject.
It's happened to me now. The harsh life I've lived up to now —
with life's race almost run — I now renounce. Why?
 I've discovered from this business that nothing is better          860
for a man than to be easy-going and open-minded.
Anyone can easily see this looking at my brother and me.
He's lived his life at leisure, in happy company,
open-minded, calm, offending no one to his face, a smile for everyone.
He's lived for himself, he spent his money on himself.
Everyone speaks well of him, everyone loves him.
I'm from the country, tough, grim,
thrifty, hot-headed, tenacious, married. What misery!
Sons were born, more trouble.
Whoa, in my zeal to provide for them the best I could,
I ground down the best years of my life in the struggle.
Now my life completed, the reward I get from them for my labors: 870
everyone hates me. My brother, without working for it,
enjoys all the pleasures of being a father.
They love him, they run away from me.
They confide all their plans to him, they have affection for him,
they both live at his house, I'm left alone.
They want a long life for him;
they look forward for me to die, I think.

To bring them up cost me all my work
and he has made them his at no expense.
I endure the misery; he enjoys the pleasures.
 Alright, now let's try the opposite.
See if I am capable of gracious speech and kindly act.
It's his challenge. I want to be loved and valued by my family.
If that can happen by my being generous                          880
and giving people what they want
and telling them what they want to hear,
I will play the leading part.
There won't be enough money,
but what do I care? I'm the oldest.

*(Syrus enters from the house. Delivery changes to unaccompanied speech.)*

**SYRUS**

Hey, Demea, your brother doesn't want you so far away.

**DEMEA**

Who is this? O my good Syrus, hello.
What's going on? How are you doing?

**SYRUS**

Well, fine.

**DEMEA**

Wonderful!
*(to himself)* Already I've added three unnatural phrases
to my vocabulary: "O my good Syrus,"
"What's going on?" and " How are you doing?"
Even though you're a slave,
you demonstrate some refinement
and I would be happy to do you a favor.

**SYRUS**

Well, thank you.

**DEMEA**

And Syrus, I really mean it as you will soon find out.

*(Geta enters from Sostrata's house.)*

**GETA**

*(inside)* Mistress, I'll go over and find out
how soon they'll be receiving the bride.                          890

Hello, Demea. My greetings.

**DEMEA**

Hello, ah, what is your name?

**GETA**
Geta.

**DEMEA**
Geta, I have formed the opinion
that you are a most valuable person.
In my view, the slave that is tried and true
is the one who looks to his master's interest,
and I see that you are such, Geta.
For this reason, should the opportunity arise,
I would be happy to do you a favor.

*(to himself)* I'm practicing being affable,
and it's going very well.

**GETA**
You're kind to have such a good opinion of me.

**DEMEA**
*(to himself)* For the very first time,
little by little, I'm building a constituency.

*(Aeschinus enters from the house.)*

**AESCHINUS**
I'm not going to survive their attention
to every single ritual of a wedding.
They're wasting the day with the preparations.                900

**DEMEA**
How's it going, Aeschinus?

**AESCHINUS**
Ah, father, you're here.

**DEMEA**
Yes, I swear, your father in heart as well as by nature.
A father who loves you more than his own eyes.
But why aren't you bringing your wife on home?

**AESCHINUS**
I want to. But there's a delay.
We're waiting for the reed player
and the singers to sing the wedding hymn.

**DEMEA**
Listen, will you listen to an old man?

**AESCHINUS**
What?

**DEMEA**

Forget all that, the wedding hymn, the crowds,
the torches, the reed players.
Just have the garden wall between your two houses
knocked down, immediately. Bring her into your house that way.
Make one house of the two. Bring to our house her mother          910
and all her family.

**AESCHINUS**

Yes, wonderful, my dear father.

**DEMEA**

Splendid. I'm called wonderful now.
My brother's house will become a highway.
There will be crowds of people. It will cost lots of money.
What do I care? I'm wonderful. I'm now in favor.
So let that Babylonian spendthrift pay out his twenty minas now.
Syrus, why don't you go and do it?

**SYRUS**

What am I to do?

**DEMEA**

Have the garden wall demolished.

You, go over and bring them around.

**GETA**

May the gods bless you, Demea.
I see that you are a sincere benefactor to my household.

**DEMEA**

They deserve it. What do you say?

**AESCHINUS**

I agree.                                                          920

**DEMEA**

That's much better for a woman
who has just given birth and is weak
than to be led through the street.

**AESCHINUS**

I've never seen anything better, my father.

**DEMEA**

That's my way.

Well, here's Micio coming out the door.

*(Micio enters from his house.)*

**MICIO**
My brother ordered this? Where is he?
Demea, you ordered this?

**DEMEA**
I did indeed. And in this way and in every other way
I would like us to make one household as best we can:
support, assistance, joining together.

**AESCHINUS**
Yes, please, father.

**MICIO**
Well, I'm not against it.

**DEMEA**
I should think not. It's the only decent thing to do.
Now first, our boy's wife has a mother.

**MICIO**
Yes. And...

**DEMEA**
She's honest and reputable.                                           930

**MICIO**
So they say.

**DEMEA**
She's older.

**MICIO**
I know that.

**DEMEA**
For a while now beyond child-bearing years,
with no one to care for her. She's alone.

**MICIO**
(to himself) What's he got in mind?

**DEMEA**
The right thing to do is that you should marry her,
and you, Aeschinus, should see that it happens.

(Delivery changes to accompanied speech.)

**MICIO**
I should marry her?

**DEMEA**
You should.

**MICIO**
I should?

**DEMEA**
Yes, you should.

**MICIO**
You're crazy.

**DEMEA**
If you, Aeschinus, are human, he will do it.

**AESCHINUS**
Father.

**MICIO**
Why are you listening to him, you fool?

**DEMEA**
You're not accomplishing anything. There's no other way.

**MICIO**
You're mad.

**AESCHINUS**
Let me beg you, father.

**MICIO**
You're crazy, get away.

**DEMEA**
Come, grant your son's wish.

**MICIO**
Are you in your right mind?
I'm finally to become a bridegroom at the age of sixty-four
and marry a decrepit old woman?
This is what you're trying to persuade me of?

**AESCHINUS**
Do it. I promised them.                                       940

**MICIO**
You promised them? Be generous with what's yours to give, boy.

**DEMEA**
Come, what if he had asked for something bigger?

**MICIO**
There couldn't be anything bigger.

**DEMEA**
Grant his request.

**AESCHINUS**
Don't be stubborn.

**DEMEA**
Go ahead, promise.

**MICIO**
Forget it.

**DEMEA**
Not till I get what I want.

**MICIO**
This is, this is violence.

**DEMEA**
Be generous, Micio.

**MICIO**
This seems to me wrong, silly, absurd,
and entirely foreign to my way of life.
But if you want it so much, I agree.

**AESCHINUS**
Well done. Thank you.

**DEMEA**
You deserve my love. But...

**MICIO**
What? I'll marry her and that's as much as I'm willing to do.

**DEMEA**
There is Hegio to think of, their closest kinsman,
now an inlaw of ours. He is not well off.
The decent thing is to do him a favor.

**MICIO**
Do what?

**DEMEA**
Outside of town you have a small plot of land
that rents as farm land. Let's give it to him
to make some money with.                                    950

**MICIO**
A small plot you say?

**DEMEA**
If it's a large plot, still, we must do it.
He's been a father to her. He's a good man.
He's part of our family now. It's right he should have it.
Let me remind you, Micio, of something you said not too long ago:
This is our common flaw, we all care much too much about money.
We ought to avoid this stain.
You were right and we ought to realize your meaning.

**AESCHINUS**

Please, father.

**MICIO**

(*Unaccompanied.*)
Alright, the farm will be given to Hegio, since my son wishes.

**DEMEA**

I'm very happy. Now you're my brother in spirit as well as flesh.

(*Accompaniment resumes.*)
(*to himself*) I'm cutting his throat with his own sword.

(*Syrus enters from Micio's house.*)

**SYRUS**

I've taken care of what you wanted done, Demea.

**DEMEA**

Well, Syrus you're a useful man.
In my opinion at least, I vote that Syrus be made a free man.          960

**MICIO**

Made a free man? Why is that?

**DEMEA**

For many reasons.

**SYRUS**

O my friend, Demea. I swear you are a good man.
From the time they were boys, I raised your two sons
very carefully. I taught them, counseled them,
always gave them good instruction as far as I could.

**DEMEA**

That's obvious. The list goes on:
buying party supplies on credit, procuring them prostitutes,
preparing dinners in broad daylight.
These are the duties of a distinguished man.

**SYRUS**

What a wonderful man!

**DEMEA**

And finally, today, he was the facilitator
in buying that music girl. He got the job done.
It's the right thing that he profit from it.
The other slaves will be the better for it.
Besides, your son wants it.

**MICIO**

Do you desire it?

**AESCHINUS**
Yes, very much.

**MICIO**
Of course you want it. Syrus, come here to me.                    970
There, be a free man.

**SYRUS**
You have done a good thing. Thank you.
I am grateful to all of you, and especially to Demea.

**DEMEA**
I'm very happy.

**AESCHINUS**
So am I.

**SYRUS**
I'm sure you are. If only my joy could now be made complete.
I wish I could see Phrygia a free woman, together with me as my wife.

**DEMEA**
Well, she's an excellent woman.

**SYRUS**
And hers was the first breast
to nurse your son's son, your grandson.

**DEMEA**
In all seriousness, by Heracles,
seeing as how she was the first nurse of my grandson,
there's no doubt that the right thing
is to emancipate her.

**MICIO**
For that?

**DEMEA**
For that. Here, let me reimburse you for what she's worth.

**SYRUS**
May all the gods bestow on you, Demea,
everything that you pray for.

**MICIO**
Well, Syrus, you've done very nicely today.

**DEMEA**
Only if you do your duty, Micio,
and extend him a little something to live on.                    980
I'm sure he will pay it back to you soon.

**MICIO**

I won't give him anything.

**AESCHINUS**

He's a good man.

**SYRUS**

I'll pay it back, I swear, if you give me anything.

**AESCHINUS**

Go ahead, father.

**MICIO**

I'll think about it.

**DEMEA**

He'll do it.

**SYRUS**

You're the best of men.

**AESCHINUS**

O my dear father, that's the spirit of the day.

**MICIO**

What is going on here?
What has caused this sudden change in your behavior?
What's this urge to give money away?
What's this generosity that's come over you?

**DEMEA**

I will tell you. I wanted to demonstrate to you
that what our children think is
easygoing and generous in you
doesn't come from sincerity or from what is right and just,
but from telling people what they want to hear,
from indulgence, from wasting money, Micio.
Now Aeschinus, if my life has been hateful to you
because I didn't go along with everything you wanted          990
wholeheartedly, right or wrong, forget it.
Squander, spend, live for whatever is your pleasure.
But if you prefer, in those areas where you lack vision
because of your youth, where your desires
are intense but your consideration is small,
to have someone to point out your fault
and correct you and indulge you at the right time,
here I am to do it for you.

**AESCHINUS**

We'll allow you, father.
You know better what we need. But what about my brother?

**DEMEA**

I'll allow it. Let him keep the girl.
But let that be the end of that sort of behavior.

**MICIO**

That's right.

**ALL**

Applause!